# Tales
## *of a*
# Turkey Farmer

by Robert W. Bitz

with illustrations by Ann Lee Yackel

LCCN: 2011916111
ISBN: 978-0-615-53698-9
First edition, published 2011.

Ward Bitz Publishing
Baldwinsville, NY

The author may be contacted at:
P.O. Box 302
Plainville, NY 13137

# Preface

Change occurs in all facets of our lives but with increasing rapidly as each year goes by. Few people have had the opportunity to see as complete a change in an industry, during one lifetime, as I have been able to observe in the turkey industry. My parents grew turkeys at the very beginning of the commercialization of the turkey industry and I was a part of it from the time I could walk.

During the 1800s and into the 1930s many farms had a small flock of turkeys, perhaps 25, maybe 50, but seldom as many as 100. Generally it was a barnyard flock with eggs hatched by the turkey hen setting on its nest. A farm might have four or five hens, each producing eight or ten poults but generally half of them died before maturity because of disease or predators. Several thousand turkeys on one farm was very unusual. My parents were pioneers in commercial turkey production and both my son and I continued the pioneering spirit by producing new turkey products, improved processing procedures and developing cutting edge methods.

The stories I relate in this book are all things that actually happened. They are old stories because the greater the passage of time between past and present the richer the perspective. Perhaps they remain imbedded in my mind because of tremendous changes in which I have been a player.

Turkeys always provided me with more enjoyment than any of the numerous other agricultural commodities that I was familiar with. Actually it wasn't the turkeys that attracted me as much as it was the opportunity to create my own destiny. Growing animals or crops to sell to someone else, to process and market, had no appeal. By performing the processing and marketing services we could not only add profit but could also take credit for outstanding quality. We could also make rapid adjustments when the product didn't measure up to customers' expectations.

My parents taught me the joy of hard work and doing it well. I feel blessed to have had many wonderful opportunities that work with turkeys provided. During my working years I have been blessed to have many fine people working at my side. Much of what was accomplished was due to their diligent efforts. Seldom do I mention names because, without question many worthy people would be overlooked. In addition, the experiences mentioned occurred so long ago that most of the people involved are gone.

I hope the reader will enjoy reading about the old days on a turkey farm and perhaps get a chuckle or two for their effort.

# Acknowledgments

L ife is composed of one's many experiences, often triggered by people
or closely associated with people. The stories in this book deviate from
normal experiences in that they deal around my association with turkeys.
For a person born and living on a farm it is not unusual to have lifelong
experiences with a specific animal species. It is rather uncommon, however
to have it with the turkey.

Perhaps, in the future I will write of a more varied variety of lifetime
experiences but the centerpiece of our American Thanksgiving and our
'almost national emblem' take center stage at the moment. There are, of
course, supporting actors in the form of people and animals to permit the
turkey to have the lead role.

I am thankful for the guidance, discipline and strong work ethic passed
on to me by my parents. In addition I want to thank the hundreds of people
who have worked at my side, growing, processing and marketing Plainville
turkeys during these past 70 years. The work, many times, was far from
being fun but by working together we produced a product of which we
were proud and that was enjoyed by the consumer.

I have only a few pictures depicting turkey growing in the past. We
had little time to stop and take pictures but the major reason that they
are limited is that what we were doing was a part of normal day-to-day
activities, so why bother. To help fill this void I am indebted to Ann Yackel
for her clever drawings depicting aspects of many of the stories I have
related in this book.

While reading the stories in this book I hope the reader, especially
anyone under the age of 50 who might explore these pages, will not only

gain a little understanding of turkeys but also how rapidly the turkey industry has changed during one lifetime. The changes in almost any business, agriculture or other, would parallel the rapidity of change in the turkey industry.

# Tales of a Turkey Farmer

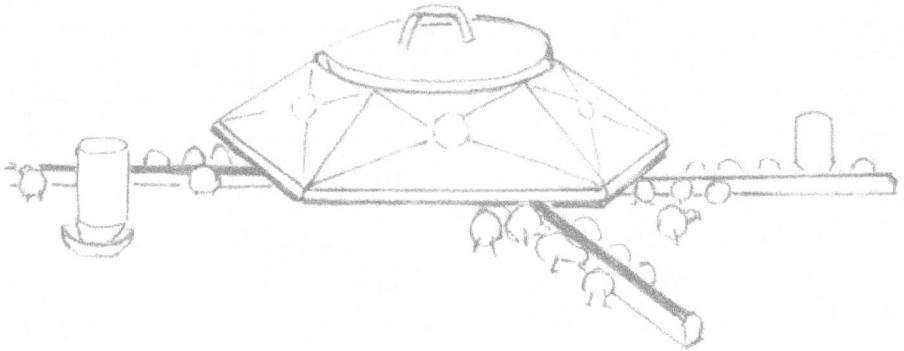

# Life for a Plainville Turkey in the 1940s

When we arrived at the Post Office, Poult and his companions greeted us with a loud chorus of "peep-peep-peep". They were suffering from travel fatigue and ready for a good meal and some room to run around. Soon Poult and his companions were deposited in a brooder house, a small building designed to replicate the responsibilities of Hen along with more than a dozen of her sisters. There was a big warm brooder stove in the middle of the building and a variety of containers, scattered in the building, providing a convenient supply of food and water.

Poult's food was not the normal bugs and grass, however, but just one mixture of many ingredients. Vitamins, minerals, protein and calories were all combined into one healthy food, so Poult would be even bigger than if he had stayed with Hen.

Poult led a life of leisure. He was provided with all the food and water he wanted and it was available any time he wanted it. It was an even better life than that of his owner. Poult's owner not only had to work, but he also had to pay taxes. Poult didn't even worry about paying taxes.

As Poult and his companions rapidly grew they were provided with more room and a regularly changing food designed to provide the exact nutrients needed for best growth. There was no candy or soda and at his teenage equivalent years, there was no exploration into smoking or drugs. There was no "junk food" for Poult!

When Poult and his companions were eight weeks old, they were moved from the security of a small building to an open field of grass, where they had lots of room to run and even to practice some flying. They didn't fly very high but managed to fly over the five-foot fence that surrounded the field. No matter how hard they tried, they could never fly back into the field. Every morning and night, when we came to feed them, we opened the gate in the fence and herded them back in. It was a good thing we did because if we hadn't, Mr. Fox would have had a sumptuous meal during the night.

Now that he was in an open field, Poult had his first taste of bugs, grass and grasshoppers. They were all good, but we made certain that Poult always had plenty of good nutritious food to eat. We even made trips to the creamery and brought back barrels of skim milk for Poult and his friends to enjoy. We took a pail and spread the skim milk on top of the containers that held Poult's food. Poult and his friends would run to the feeders, almost knocking us over in their rush to enjoy their food covered with skim milk. It was delicious! It was literally "the frosting on the cake".

One day several of us came to the field with some large empty boxes, instead of the usual large bags of food. Poult and his friends, now only a few months old, have become mature toms and hens, ready for an unknown next step in life. They wondered what we were going to do with those boxes? What new experiences will Poult and his friends, who are now toms and hens, have? Perhaps they will have a free ride to a new destination with a much warmer environment.

*Circa 1943. We are using a telescoping pen to catch and crate turkeys for processing. In the background, on the right is the tobacco shed where the turkeys were processed. The other barns housed the cows and horses.*

# Trips to the Feed Mill

We did not have our own feed mill on the farm until the 1960s, so from the time I learned to walk, I often accompanied my dad to Cayuga, 30 miles away, to purchase turkey feed from Beacon Milling Company. The mill was a fascinating place for a small boy. Unfamiliar noises from the milling machines, the pungent smell of warm molasses and the huge buildings on the shore of Cayuga Lake combined to make it seem like another world.

Bulk feed was unheard of at this time, so all of the feed was put in white cotton bags that each held 100 pounds. Dad's truck seemed big to me but five tons was the maximum sized load it could haul. Dad backed his truck up to the loading dock and several men would bring the bags to a conveyer and the feed was loaded on the truck. Back home the feed was unloaded and piled to await use, as the turkeys always needed feed. Ironically one of the places it was stored was in the living room of the house where, later, my wife and I lived as bride and groom for over 50 years.

My sister Ruth was six years my elder. When she became 16, in 1940, she obtained her driver's license. Both of us, from an early age, were expected to be part of the farm's labor force whenever there was a need. It was natural for my dad to say one morning, "Ruth, you can take the truck to Cayuga and pick up a load of turkey feed this afternoon."

My sister was an attractive young lady and didn't relish the idea of going to the mill by herself to deal with all the workmen eyeing her up and down. She indicated the same to her father and he replied, "Bob can go with you to take care of the paperwork and see that the feed is loaded properly." As a result, my sister and I became a team to draw turkey feed from the Beacon Milling Company to the farm during the summer months.

Ruth backed the truck up to the dock at the feed mill and stayed in the truck while I handled the paper work and saw that the bags of feed were piled appropriately. If the weather was rainy or threatening I would tie a waterproof canvas over the feed and we would head for home. Since I was too small to handle the 100-pound bags of feed, Dad unloaded the truck each time we returned home.

We were fortunate to never have had a flat tire or a truck breakdown on our trips and the brother and sister team operated successfully. The truck had to chug pretty hard going up some big hills but my sister was in complete control.

*Circa 1943. Turkeys soon to be dressed for marketing. There are two tobacco boxes on the wagon holding the large toms. The smaller crates on the back held the hens. The tractor is a 1939 Farmall International purchased in 1939. It was the farm's first tractor but horses were still actively used. From left to right; Harry Bitz, Bob Bitz (partially hidden), Winthrop Van Camp, Ralph Vaughn*

# A Surprise

"We're going to get you tonight, Grandpap," chuckled Harley.

"Yes, you had better nail your bed to the floor and tie yourself in it or you'll have a big bump on your head tomorrow morning," chimed in Charley.

Grandpap was a lovable old fellow, not really that old, probably around 50, but old in the minds of the jovial teenagers who loved to tease him. Grandpap, the father of nine, earned a little extra money for his family by sleeping with the turkeys. Yes, that's right, sleeping with the turkeys. Back in the 1930s, it was not uncommon for an irresponsible derelict to make a nighttime foray into a flock of domestic turkeys and make off with some of them. Grandpap was provided with a little shanty, containing a cot, where he could sleep. When a predator inadvertently aroused the sleeping turkeys, they would scatter in all directions and make a noisy ruckus. Grandpap, awakened by the noise of the turkeys, would jump out of bed and armed with his shotgun, make a quick move to accost and remove any ill-advised visitor of the night.

"We're going to pick up one side of your shanty tonight, with you inside, and roll it over," Earl enthusiastically added.

It was Halloween and boys in the country enjoyed playing tricks, sometimes a bit overdone. A few years earlier, a missing buggy owned by one of the neighbors was found resting comfortably on the top of the local schoolhouse. The morning after Halloween it was common practice to find the outhouses in the community lying on their sides, with their unseemly contents exposed and unusual pungent odors drifting through the air.

Grandpap smiled and responded to the banter. "You'd better be careful boys, I've loaded my shotgun shells with rock salt and I don't miss! If you get a little of that under your hides it'll hurt more than any of the lickins your pa ever gave you."

Grandpap and the boys went back to their various chores and nothing more was said until the following morning when Grandpap accosted the boys. "Where did you rascals disappear to last night? About two in the morning I felt you jokesters trying to tip over my shanty. I was outside in a flash with my shotgun in hand but none of you were to be seen. It was a full moon and you couldn't disappear into thin air."

"We never went near your shanty last night," replied Charley. "We were in our beds before ten. You must have been dreaming. Wha'd you do, nip the bottle a little too much last night?"

"You know darn well I didn't hit the bottle," replied Grandpap. "You boys must have been out there horsin around!"

"Grandpap got fooled," shouted Harley. "About two last night our house shook and this morning the radio said we had an earthquake."

*A turkey education conference at Plainville Turkey Farm in 1936. Harry Bitz is explaining how turkeys are prepared for customers. The people listening to him are other turkey growers from NY State. The small door on the left opens to the tobacco stripping room where the turkeys were prepared for marketing.*

# Milk, Yum-Yum

F ancy milk-fed turkeys! Yes, that was the by-line on the Plainville Turkey Farm sign for many years. When it comes to milk we think of mammals, not birds, but Plainville turkeys loved their milk.

Turkeys in the wild subsist on insects, bugs, worms, nuts, berries and seeds. Wild turkeys seem to have one eye looking for food while the other eye searches for predators, such as foxes and hawks, that can appear without notice to make off with an impromptu turkey dinner.

Since domestic turkeys don't have the opportunity to scrounge the countryside in search of food, man must provide food for them. Seventy years ago, turkey nutrition was in its infancy and the turkey farmer experimented with a variety of feedstuffs to combine fast growth with tasty and tender meat for eating. The standard feeds were oats, wheat, corn and barley. Fishmeal or meat scrap was added to provide sufficient protein for good growth. One had to be careful about using fishmeal the last few weeks before marketing the turkeys, however, as the customer would notice a strong fish flavor in the turkey.

In the 1930s and 1940s, most people were very active physically, drinking whole milk and enjoying thick slabs of butter on their bread. Calories were needed, with few people becoming fat, and almost no one at that time would consider drinking skim milk. Since the butterfat was removed from whole milk and used to make butter there was a great deal of inexpensive skim milk remaining. Dad knew that milk was good for children and he reasoned that it would be good for growing turkeys. He was right and grew some of the best turkeys there were.

My dad loaded several empty wooden barrels, with one end knocked out, on his truck and twice a week headed for the creamery to have them filled with skim milk. An empty bag, fastened with a barrel hoop was placed over the barrel's open end to keep the milk from slopping out when he went over bumps in the road.

Some people think turkeys are dumb, but sometimes they seem to know more than humans. We fed the turkeys cafeteria-style. There were a number of wooden feed troughs and a different feed was put in each; oats in one, wheat in another, corn in another and mash, which was a mix of vitamins, minerals, meat scrap and other ingredients in another. The turkeys would eat only as much as they needed from each trough without over indulging on any one feed.

Since the mash was dry, we poured the skim milk on the mash, which readily absorbed it. If we were to pour the milk on the whole grain it would flow to the bottom of the trough and sour before the turkeys ate it. Pouring the skim milk on the dry mash was like giving candy to a child. The turkeys loved it and crowded around the feed trough, each one trying to eat more of the milk than the other. Little did they realize that the delicious milk was taking them a step closer to providing some lucky family with a delicious turkey dinner!

*Circa 1952. Charles Green, a long time employee, is scalding a turkey in 200+ degree water prior to removing the feathers. This picture was taken in a new cement block building that had replaced the old tobacco stripping room. Mr. Green was an outstanding employee who lived and worked on the farm for over 30 years.*

# A Rapid Weight Gain

Sometimes you can drive turkeys in groups, similar to driving cattle, and other times, well, you cannot. One day, back in the 1930s, when domestic turkeys were long and lean and could fly as well as wild turkeys, we were driving a flock of turkeys to the processing plant. Somewhat, like a child, when you want it to exhibit good behavior, turkeys have a mind of their own. This particular day they chose not to cooperate.

We were nearing the processing plant, when all of a sudden, one of the turkeys was spooked by some unknown object. The turkey took off like a jet on an airport runway. The rest of the flock seemed to have thought that flying was a good idea and took off in every direction. Immediately, where the turkeys had been, nothing remained but a few feathers floating in the air.

We started gathering a few turkeys here and a few there, gradually bringing them back into some semblance of order and gently herded them into a barn adjacent to the processing plant. Breathing a sigh of relief, for successfully completing the task, we headed toward the house to enjoy some well-earned lunch.

Coming out of the house one of the men happened to look up and exclaimed, "Three of those stupid turkeys are in the top of those trees." We all looked up and near the tops of two of the large maple trees in the front yard three turkeys were comfortably resting. We all wondered how we were going to get the turkeys out of the trees since they were up high, too far to climb. One of the men had recently played football and still had the football in his car. As he went to get it, he proudly stated, "I'll knock those birds right out of the trees."

He took good aim and let the football fly toward the turkeys. To watch those turkeys you would think they were big football fans, sitting on the 50-yard line watching a big game. He kept throwing the football at the turkeys to no avail. One time it came real close to a turkey and the turkey ducked as the football went flying by. The other men also tried to throw the football, none with any success. Finally my dad said, "Let the fool things sit there all night. I'll put some corn under the trees and by morning they'll be hungry and come down for the corn."

The next morning the turkeys were still in the trees, apparently not sufficiently interested in the corn to fly down. Dad said, "I'll fix them," as he went in the house to get his shotgun. Two shots later, three turkeys came tumbling down out of the trees. They were immediately taken to the processing plant, throats cut and prepared for sale.

A few days later we got a call from a customer saying, "I drove out to your farm to purchase a farm grown turkey last Monday and you passed off a wild turkey on me."

My dad responded, "Absolutely not, all of our turkeys are raised here on our farm."

"Don't feed me that kind of baloney," the customer responded, "I almost broke a tooth on a piece of buckshot!"

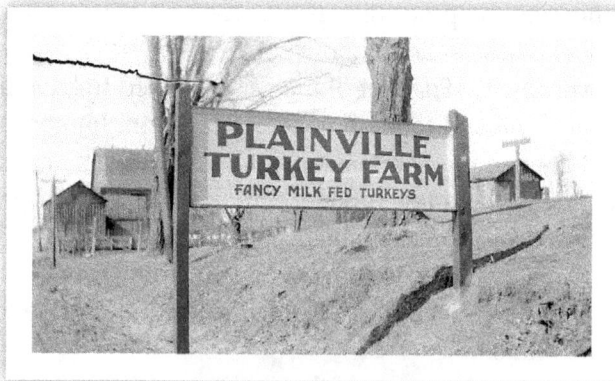

*Circa 1936. This sign stood in front of the farm for many years promoting our 'Fancy Milk Fed Turkeys". The sign hides the tobacco shed, where the turkeys were processed.*

# Tobacco Boxes and Turkeys

How could tobacco boxes have anything to do with turkeys? In the 1930s and 40s, at Plainville Turkey Farm, tobacco boxes were similar to the duct tape of today. We put them to many uses.

The boxes were rectangular wooden boxes slightly less than four feet by three feet by three feet. They were constructed of high quality, full inch soft pine lumber and designed for shipping leaf tobacco. We purchased these boxes by the truckload for a good price, from a chewing tobacco manufacturer in Syracuse.

When a truckload of boxes arrived at the farm we saved a few to turn into large turkey crates for hauling live turkeys from the fields to the processing plant. Two handholds were cut in each side near the bottom of the box. The loose boards that had once been its top were cut and fitted to provide a door large enough to pass live turkeys through. The boxes were heavy to begin with and when five live turkeys, weighing 30 pounds each, were put inside, it took two strong men to lift each box.

Some of the other uses of the boxes were for the storage of used feedbags, a cover for a centrifugal pump and as a sales counter for dressed turkeys. Prior to every Thanksgiving, Christmas and New Year holiday, and sometimes in between, we took fresh dressed turkeys to sell at the Central NY Regional Market in Syracuse. Two of these tobacco boxes were laid on one side with the open top facing the sales people making a perfect sales counter. Brown tobacco paper was placed on top of the boxes and the dressed turkeys were laid out on top of the paper. There was no covering over the turkeys, so they were exposed to whatever germs and dust might float through the air. It seems crude today, but many thousands of fresh turkeys were sold from the top of these boxes, over a 40-year span.

Most of the boxes were dismantled for their lumber. The lumber had many uses including constructing 12 by 14-foot brooder houses. The boards were nailed to a framework, covering floor, ceiling and sides. Three windows were placed in the building and then it was covered with tarpaper making an economical and functional building that lasted for years.

Surplus lumber from the boxes was stored in a barn until it was needed for various small jobs around the farm. As a boy, I had many hours of enjoyment sawing boards and pounding nails making the wonderful things only a young boy can dream of.

The lumber sold today does not begin to match the quality of the lumber that went into making boxes for shipping tobacco in the 1930s. The beautiful virgin timber that was used for the tobacco boxes then has all but disappeared. If lumber like that was available today, it would likely cost more than 100 times what we paid for the lumber in those tobacco shipping boxes.

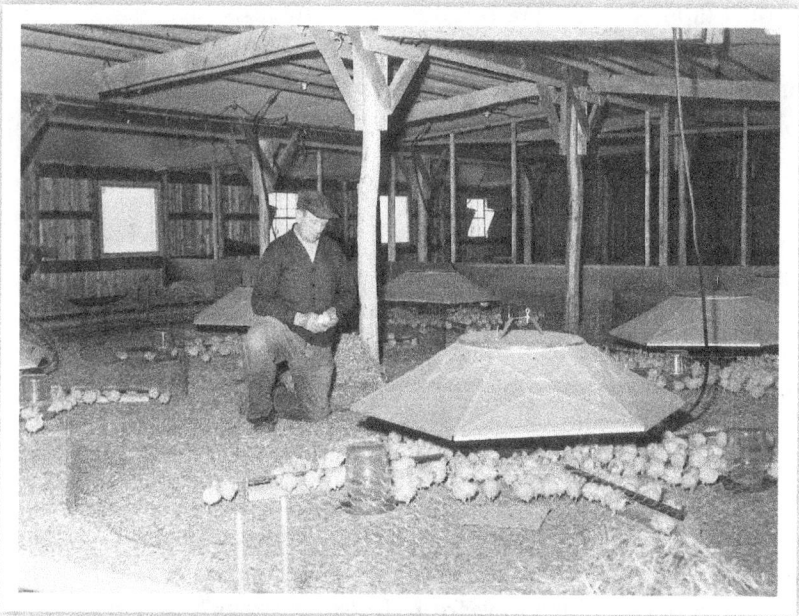

*Circa 1954. Harry Bitz (the author's father) is shown holding a day-old turkey poult in the new brooder building constructed in 1954. Note the wire ring around each brooder stove and the feeders and waterers. You can also see several of the locust poles that were used in the building's structure.*

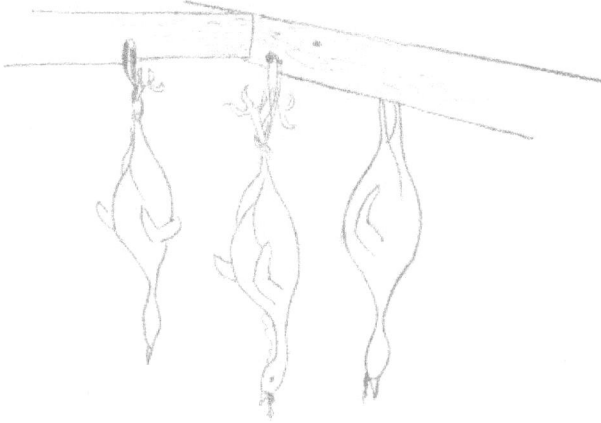

# Hanging Turkeys in the Cellar

Until after World War II, almost no turkey farm had a controlled environment for its dressed turkeys. Once the turkeys were slaughtered, the temperature of their meat was at the mercy of the weather. The turkeys had to be processed when they were of appropriate size and when the customers wanted them. In the northeastern United States, the weather was usually cold enough to refrigerate a turkey hanging outside during late November and December.

If there was a warm spell, it was essential that the live turkeys not be slaughtered before the day they were delivered to the customer. A turkey farmer prayed for cool weather the weeks before Thanksgiving and Christmas to help keep the birds fresh.

If dressed turkeys had to be kept on the farm overnight, what could a turkey grower do if there was unusually cold weather, sometimes 20 degrees below zero, the week before Christmas? He couldn't let the turkeys freeze or his customers would refuse to accept them. At Plainville Turkey Farm, the solution was to hang the dressed turkeys from nails driven in the floor joists of the cellar in the family home. Since the turkeys still had their feet attached a string was placed around their legs and they were transported to the cellar.

The most convenient method of transporting the turkeys was on a pair of bobs, a flat-bottomed sleigh with double runners on each end. (That is why it was called a pair of bobs. I believe they were called bobs because the runners tended to bob up and down as the sleigh traveled over snow drifts and bumps of ice.) A team of horses was hooked to the bobs, and a couple of horse blankets were laid on the flat bottom to keep the turkeys clean. The bobs had probably been used to haul cow manure to the field earlier in the day. The turkeys were carefully laid on its flat bottom and hauled by the horses about 500 feet to the house.

At the house a couple of boys were delegated to carry the turkeys, one by one, down the cellar steps to my dad who hung them on the nails in the ceiling. The temperature in the cellar was in the 40s so the turkeys wouldn't freeze. The next morning, the turkeys were carried up out of the cellar and put on the truck for delivery. Since it was still very cold outside, the turkeys were covered with horse blankets and then with a canvas to prevent them from freezing while being delivered.

The butcher at the store was happy because the turkeys weren't frozen. He now had the job of removing the head, feet, viscera and giblets from the turkeys prior to delivering them to his customers. An interesting side note: the turkeys were weighed and priced before losing all of their parts. The customer paid for a 15-pound turkey, which would have actually weighed about 12 pounds when it was purchased. There was opportunity for a dishonest butcher to pad the turkey's weight.

*Circa 1937. Arthur Hudson, a partner in the 1930s turkey growing business with my dad, is shown moving a bobs sleigh load of turkeys from the tobacco shed to hang in the cellar of the house to keep the turkeys from freezing during the night. The house shown has been home to the author and his wife for over 50 years and was constructed by the author's great-great grandfather in 1835. On the right is a horse. In 1937, all farm power was provided by man and horse. The turkeys shown are NY dressed with only blood and feathers removed.*

# Feathers

If you grow and process turkeys, you have feathers to contend with. They must be removed from the bird before it is cooked. For centuries, the normal procedure was to bleed the bird and then immediately pull the feathers from the carcass in their dry natural state. The feathers did not release easily from the feather follicles making their removal a difficult task. Standard practice was to leave some of the long wing feathers attached to the wings. This is still commonly done where a person grows only a few turkeys for their own use and in countries where turkey production is limited. I can remember visiting the meat department in Harrods Department Store in London, in the 1980s, where the premium turkeys sold still had their wing feathers attached.

Today, large commercial turkey processing plants scald the birds in water at a temperature of 140 degrees. This water temperature loosens the feathers so that mechanical pickers, with long rubber fingers, can easily brush the feathers from the turkeys. Kosher dressed turkeys are required to be scalded at a lower temperature, making it more difficult to remove the feathers.

During the 1930s and 1940s Plainville Turkey Farm pulled the more valuable feathers from the turkeys, immediately after bleeding, before they were scalded. Once the turkeys are scalded the feathers lose their value. The feathers were pulled by the handful with the long wing and tail feathers placed in one bag and the finer body feathers in another bag.

Turkey feathers are too coarse to use as filling for pillows. They were largely used for decorative purposes on novelty items. Only the white feathers had value as they could be dyed whatever color a person wanted. I remember seeing gorgeous ladies gowns, totally covered with turkey feathers, offered for sale in the 1980s.

Shortly after the Christmas holiday, my dad would receive two or three phone calls from feather buyers in New York City. The high bidder traveled by train to Syracuse where he hired a taxi to come to our farm 20 miles away. It was an unusual experience for me because, previously I had never seen a taxi outside the city of Syracuse. The feather merchant examined some of the bags of feathers, and once he approved several bags were weighed at a time on steelyards, a simple balance scale that had been used to weigh products for thousands of years.

After weighing, the feather merchant reached in his pocket and paid for the feathers with cash. It seemed to me like a lot of money, usually several hundred dollars. A normal price was about 25 cents a pound for the large feathers and 50 cents a pound for the smaller body feathers. There were usually about one thousand pounds, which represented millions of feathers.

As our turkey business grew it was not convenient or profitable to save the feathers. Sometimes we delegated a person to pluck wing and tail feathers to give to visiting schoolchildren. Large turkey and chicken plants, that have a large volume of feathers, turn them into a valuable high protein feed ingredient that is often used in pet food.

Circa 1954. This picture, of turkeys being plucked by hand, was taken in the new turkey processing building. The methods, for the first two years, were the same as were used in the old tobacco stripping room. Notice the wooden tub to collect water from the nearby pail used clean the turkeys after plucking. Left to right are Peg Pickard, Tom McGovern, Willard Whorral and Nellie Green, all fine neighbors who helped us pluck turkeys prior to Thanksgiving and Christmas.

# Prisoners of War on the Farm

In 1943, I was a boy of 13 and very impressed when German prisoners of war came to work on our farm. Farm labor was very scarce because of the millions of young Americans in the armed forces, coupled with millions of older men and women working in plants producing a multitude of products for the war effort. The production of agricultural goods was critical for the war effort and some young American farmers were deferred from military service to produce food on the farm. German prisoners of war were stationed at a number of strategic locations in New York State and were used to help alleviate the shortage of farm labor.

At Howland's Island, about 25 miles from our farm, there was a prisoner of war camp. After substantiating our need and receiving approval, arrangements were made with the prison camp authorities for us to pick up prisoners and bring them to our farm. The first year of the program eight prisoners was the minimum number we could obtain. My dad drove his truck, with bushel crates on the back for the prisoners to sit on, while the guard rode in the cab with him. Each morning, when they were needed, Dad picked them up at the camp and returned them at night. Food was sent from the camp with the prisoners. My mother supplemented their food with extra sandwiches and coffee, which they appreciated.

The prisoners had never worked on a farm so they had to be delegated tasks that didn't require experience. All of the prisoners were required to work in close proximity to each other, within sight of the guard. In addition to lack of experience, the prisoners were not used to hard, physical work and were not capable of performing as much work as our regular employees. Another challenge was our inability to speak German and their inability to speak English. Communication was with rough sign language. If a prisoner needed to relieve himself, he did it on the spot since there were no portable toilets at that time.

Being a guard was a real soft job since the prisoners were happy to be in the United States and not fighting in the war. The guard's presence was more for appearance rather than need.

The prisoners did only a minimal amount of work with the turkeys. Instead, they helped pick up potatoes and bunch red kidney beans, permitting the regular employees to spend more time with the turkeys.

In 1944, the prisoners were transported to the farm without a guard. Experience had proven that they were not going to try to escape. Because a guard wasn't needed, the prison permitted a farmer to pick up as few as four prisoners and my dad delegated my mother to take the family car to pick up and return the prisoners. Although she did not enjoy doing this, she never had any problems.

It was interesting to realize that the common German soldier had no more desire for the war than the young men of the United States. The misguided German leadership was responsible for the war and the death of hundreds of thousands of innocent people.

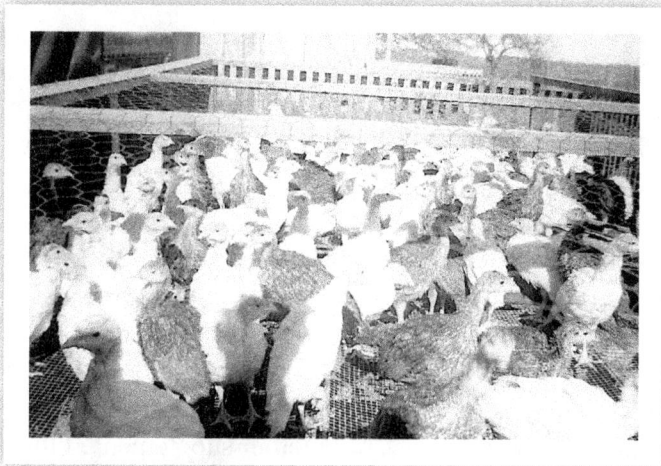

*Circa 1950. Seven-week old turkeys on a sun porch that is connected to one of the small brooding houses. The wire floor is two feet off the ground and the turkeys are able to go in and out of the brooder house. From three weeks of age until they were moved to pasture at 8 weeks, the turkeys were fed and watered on the porch.*

# The Origination of Turkeys

Where did the turkey come from? A joker would say from the egg but a more informative answer would be that it probably evolved in Central America. Both Columbus and later Spanish explorers, in the late 15$^{th}$ and early 16$^{th}$ centuries, found numerous turkeys in the New World. Montezuma, the Aztec King, had domesticated turkeys and the Spanish took some back to Europe with them. Turkeys were popular in Europe and gradually became fairly common throughout the Continent. A recipe regarding the preparation of turkey was printed in an English cookbook in 1586.

When the Pilgrims set out for the new world, we are told there were turkeys on the Mayflower. I question if that was the case but we do know that the Pilgrims received some turkeys from England for breeding stock in 1629. Whether the turkeys that supposedly were sent with the Pilgrims arrived intact or in their stomachs is not recorded. There were wild turkeys scattered throughout much of what is now the United States long before the Pilgrims arrived. Farmers learned that if they could find a wild turkey's nest and remove the eggs to hatch under one of their chicken hens, they could improve their domestic turkeys by crossing them with the wild stock.

For many years, domestic turkeys, grown in this country, were driven to the city similarly to the cattle drives in the West. Drovers purchased hundreds of turkeys from farmers and gathered them together for the turkey drive. A wagon loaded with corn and pulled by horses traveled the road ahead of the turkeys. A little corn was scattered in the road to keep the turkeys following the wagon. At night the wagon would stop in a secluded forested area with a stream nearby and the turkeys would be fed corn. After eating the corn the turkeys flew into the trees to spend the night. The drovers could move the turkeys five to eight miles a day in this manner. When the flock arrived at the city the various butchers would buy the turkeys, dress them and sell them to the residents of the city. Many of the turkeys were sold alive to housewives who would slaughter and prepare the turkeys for their family's consumption.

In Colonial times, domesticated turkeys were more than food. Turkeys, which love insects, were often driven to a field to help remove undesirable insects. Both George Washington and Thomas Jefferson used turkeys to rid their tobacco fields of tobacco worms.

By the 1920's, wild turkeys had disappeared from much of their natural habitat in the United States due to the removal of forest land for farming. In the 1950's, the NY State Department of Environmental Conservation decided to trap wild turkeys that still existed in other states, and turn them loose in NY State. Their success exceeded their wildest dreams and now there are thousands of wild turkeys scattered throughout the state. Other states followed similar programs and now there are wild turkeys in about all of the 50 states.

*Circa 1933. This is a photograph taken by the Syracuse Post Standard of Robert Bitz and Olin Hudson. At this time Olin's father, Arthur Hudson, was a partner with William Ward, Bob's grandfather, and Harry Bitz growing the turkeys.*

# Growing Turkies in 1843

*(Information for this story was taken from the December 1843 Cultivator.)*
*(In 1843 the appropriate spelling for turkey was turkie.)*

A common way to grow turkeys in 1843 was to find a wild turkie's nest in the woods and when she had laid 8 or 10 eggs, remove them from the nest and take them to the farm to put them under a setting chicken for hatching. It was very difficult to find the nest of a wild turkey and would require many days of secret observation before the observer would be successful.

The setting chicken's eggs would be removed from her nest and then replaced with the wild turkie's eggs. It was important to keep the chicken hen and the baby turkie poults confined for about two weeks after hatching to provide an appropriate bonding period. After about two weeks they could be turned loose and the poults would follow the chicken hen all over, thinking she was their mother.

It was important for the owner to let the baby poults eat out of his hand regularly so they would become tame and lose some of the fear of man that was part of their nature. As the poults grew, they might roost on the barn or even in trees in the yard. When older they would often wander off into the woods but would return at night because they were always given some food.

If a person started out with eight turkies he would be lucky to end the season with three or four as there were always foxes, coons or owls looking for a good meal. The hens (females) would be saved to grow a flock the next year.

The following spring, the clever grower would keep the hen turkie confined in a building until late morning, which was usually after it had laid its egg, and then turn it loose. The eggs were saved until there were enough to put under a setting chicken. By removing the eggs the turkie was fooled. Instead of laying the normal number of 15, she would continue to lay as many as 30. This way a couple of chicken hens and the hen turkie could each hatch some turkies.

**Author's note:** Christopher Columbus had taken some wild turkeys back to Europe with him and turkeys had been reproduced from them for over 100 years. The American colonists arrived with some of those turkeys from Europe. Most farmers did not have access to those birds and their only way to start growing turkeys was the method described above. Often, if they had reasonable success growing turkeys, they might purchase a tom from another farmer or trade toms to improve the next flock. The incubator was not in use at this time so the chicken hen became a surrogate mother.

*Circa 1964. This is a flock of large bronze toms. We were now boning turkeys and grew this flock for further processing into turkey rolls and other turkey products. In the background are roosts and shade for the turkeys. Turkeys, especially mature toms, are curious and ran up to the fence when they saw me.*

# Man's Tricks On Turkeys

The first trick man played on Tom and Hen turkey took place nearly a century ago. He fooled them into thinking it was spring, all year long. Turkeys, like most other birds, are endowed with a sense of family planning. With the increasing length of daylight hours in springtime they become amorous due to increasing hormone flow. With the advent of electricity on the farm, man discovered that by using artificial lighting to increase the number of daylight hours, turkey family planning disappeared and eggs could be produced all year long.

Nature had designed Tom and Hen turkey with a streamlined frame, allowing them to fly high up in trees. This was a means of protecting them from wild animals that enjoyed celebrating Thanksgiving on a regular basis. Since North Americans prefer white meat over dark, man selected turkeys with the widest breasts, year after year, for breeding purposes. Soon man discovered that many of the turkey eggs were not hatching. Tom was still strutting and Hen was ready, willing and able, but poor Tom was so front heavy, with breast meat, that Olympic judges wouldn't given him more than a "3" for performance! The sad solution was, Tom became relegated to a male dormitory and Hen was impregnated by artificial insemination!

Since Hen had become a full-time egg producer and no longer allowed to set on her eggs for hatching, man devised a substitute called an incubator. The first incubators held only a hundred or two eggs, and were heated with coal or kerosene, replicating Hen's body temperature. Man initially duplicated Hen's method of turning the eggs by hand, but as incubators became larger and larger, holding thousands of eggs, they were designed to turn the eggs automatically.

Baby Poult still found its way into the world by pecking through the egg membrane and then through the hard shell. Gone were the days of coming into the world under Hen's warm fluffy feathers and almost immediately setting out to find a first meal of juicy little bugs! Nature wisely provided Poult with an in-house source of food, enough to last several days. At hatching, the yolk of the egg remained Poult's body cavity, to be absorbed gradually as a source of food during his first week.

The initial food supply, designed into Poult's body, was a boon to man in his commercialization of the turkey. Because of this built-in food supply, man could put Poult in a large cardboard box with 100 of his brothers and sisters, and ship him to a turkey farm a thousand miles from the hatchery. Poult was commonly sent by mail, during the middle of the 20th century. If it was more than a two-day trip, Poult was treated to a plane ride his very first day on earth. The plane ride for Poult, however, was similar to man's today, no free meals or cocktails!

*Circa 1966. A flock of turkeys in a pole barn. As our turkey production increased we constructed pole barns to house the turkeys. Note the large turkey feeders, which were filled weekly for the turkeys.*

# Selling Turkey Eggs

My first moneymaking adventure, as a boy, was selling turkey eggs. We kept some turkey hens for breeders but they weren't trained to lay on demand. Sometimes they started laying eggs before we wanted the eggs for hatching and other times they continued to lay eggs after we had all the eggs we needed for hatching. This was in the 1930s and incubators had replaced the need for the turkey hen to sit on the eggs for hatching. There were also occasional double-yoked eggs that could not be used for hatching that I could sell.

Many people do not realize that birds will lay eggs whether they are fertilized or not. We didn't introduce the toms to the hens until two weeks before we saved eggs for hatching. If a turkey egg had been fertilized it would not have been noticeable to the user.

The surplus eggs were an ideal way for a boy to both earn some money and gain a little experience in the free-enterprise system. As eggs became available I cleaned them and obtained some brown paper bags and a few used chicken egg cartons to put them in. Neither container was ideal for turkey eggs but they served the purpose. Although a turkey is more than twice the size of a chicken, the turkey's egg is only a little larger than an extra large chicken egg. Usually a chicken egg carton wouldn't close tightly because of the larger eggs but a rubber band around the carton solved the problem.

My dad took potatoes to the Syracuse public market on Saturdays and I joined him with the turkey eggs. Turkey eggs are covered with many small brown spots making them appear different from other eggs. Customers asked what kind of eggs they were and what they tasted like. I told them that my mother used turkey eggs in baking, whenever they were available, and that what she baked was delicious. I had to charge the same price people received for their chicken eggs since no one had used turkey eggs. Because they were larger than most chicken eggs the customer got a bargain.

Occasionally an adventurous person would buy a dozen of the eggs and the next week I actually had some repeat customers. They discovered that cracking a turkey egg was much different than cracking a chicken egg. The heavier turkey requires an egg with a stronger shell so the weight of the turkey hen won't break the shell. I think some customers had a fairly steep learning curve in cracking open a turkey egg.

Some customers would have liked to purchase turkey eggs on a regular basis. When I told them that to be profitable I would have to charge the same price for two turkey eggs as for a dozen chicken eggs they were stunned. The reason for this was that a turkey only lays one-third as many eggs as a chicken and eats twice as much feed. Upon hearing this their interest in purchasing turkey eggs immediately ceased.

*Circa 1950. Richard Doback is hand feeding six-week old turkeys on a sunporch connected to a small brooder house. The trough will be placed on the wire floor of the sunporch. The feed was moved from house to house on the wheelbarrow.*

# Market

Markets have been a means of uniting producer and consumer for thousands of years. I come from a family of farmers who marketed part of their production at the Syracuse public market for about 100 years. Originally, potatoes were the product our farm marketed. Grandfather started for the market, 20 miles away, with a team of horses hitched to a wagon holding about 30 bushels of potatoes at 11:00 p.m. to arrive at the market when it opened at 5:00 a.m. the next morning. He arrived back at the farm that evening with about $18 from the sale of his potatoes. This $18 paid for his seed, fertilizer and labor to grow the crop and take it to market.

My mother told an interesting market story about when she was at the market with her father on November 11, 1918 at 11:00 a.m. It was the end of World War I and church bells rang, horns blew and firecrackers banged, scaring their horses badly.

Potatoes were the means by which our farm started growing turkeys. In 1923, my dad and grandfather were selling potatoes at the market prior to Thanksgiving. A farmer, who came a greater distance to the market, was selling live turkeys and had eight turkeys remaining that he had been unable to sell and didn't want to take home. My dad and grandfather purchased them, brought them back to the farm, fed them and took them back to the market for sale at Christmas. Apparently they were successful as they started growing turkeys on our farm the following year and sold turkeys at the market for the next 50 years.

Dad and grandfather processed the turkeys they took to market by removing the blood, feathers and intestines. Gradually they developed a clientele that looked for their turkeys and purchased them each year. As a boy of six I started to go to the market and help sell the turkeys, learning not only to sell but also a lot about human nature. At the market we had the opportunity to interact with immigrants from all over the world. I couldn't always understand them but that wasn't necessary as long as the good American dollar passed from buyer to seller. It provided a good opportunity to learn bargaining as most customers at that time tried to purchase at a lower price than asked.

There were also a variety of types of customers at the market. Until the 1950s, supermarkets were almost unknown. There were dozens, even hundreds of small stores scattered throughout Syracuse and its surrounding area. Each morning many of these storeowners would come to the market to fill their needs for the day. In addition, there were hucksters, first with horse and wagon and later with small open trucks, purchasing fruits and vegetables to peddle in various Syracuse neighborhoods. Besides these retailers there were individuals that came on foot, bus or by car to fill their needs at the market.

As the turkey business grew, my dad needed to stay on the farm to process the turkeys. He recruited two fine neighboring farmers to take our turkeys to market. I was assigned to help them and we had a lot of fun, even though they were 30 years older than me. It is ironical that 30 years later my son also had the opportunity to enjoy the same experience with these two fine gentlemen.

As our turkey business continued to grow, 1972 was our last year at the Syracuse public market. It provided both my son and myself with many fine learning experiences as well as a market to help grow our business. Occasionally I stop at the market and am pleased to note new entrepreneurs, hopefully heading toward success, getting their start at the market.

# Mother's Contribution

Often when I needed something, as a boy and even later as a man, my mother provided it. It might be a button, safety pin, or an answer to a question. She was usually able to fill my request. Since my house was less than 100 feet from my parents I often stopped in to say hello.

We weren't poor on the turkey farm but money was scarce. There always seemed to be more uses for money than what was available. In the 50s and 60s when I was growing the business and venturing into further processing of turkeys, it was often a case of make-do with whatever was available.

When we started packaging turkeys and turkey products in plastic bags, it was desirable to vacuum the bag with the turkey in it, so the bag would fit tightly around the turkey, improving its appearance. A vacuum packaging machine could be purchased for $1,000 but that was money I didn't have and it would have been inappropriate to borrow the money for a new venture that might not be necessary.

Mother had recently purchased a new vacuum cleaner so I asked her if I could borrow her old cleaner. She was willing, so I took the cleaner to the dressing plant and used the hose that extended from it, which was designed to clean furniture and small crannies, to draw a vacuum on the plastic turkey bags. After the air was removed we twisted the end of the bag and put a small rubber band over the end to seal it. The cleaner was noisy but it worked and we used it for a couple of years.

I knew the cleaner wouldn't last forever and I needed to draw a vacuum so I continued to search for an alternative. A salesman told me that the Wegman's store in Rochester had purchased two vacuum machines but was only using one. He suggested I call them and see if I could make a deal. My call was successful as I was able to purchase the machine at half price and made a deal to swap some frozen turkeys for it. I delivered the turkeys to Wegmans and picked up the vacuum machine. It provided an extra bonus as a clipping mechanism was part of the machine and we didn't have to bother with rubber bands any more.

My mother solved my initial problem and by waiting for opportunity I was able to save a substantial amount of money. Reflecting on how things have worked out in my turkey business over the years, two thoughts came to mind. Cautiousness in spending money and innovation were two factors that allowed Plainville Turkey Farm to survive and grow during a period when almost all other small turkey farms were going out of business. Mother's contribution saved the day!

*Circa 1970. This is an aerial view of the farm showing turkeys on pasture and in pole barns. One barn is shown under construction. Until 1990 we did most of the building construction with our farm labor. Eventually all of the turkeys were grown in buildings because of disease transmitted from wild birds to the turkeys on pasture.*

# The Thanksgiving Holiday

Our tradition of Thanksgiving, in the United States, dates back to the Pilgrims of the Massachusetts Colony in 1621. A successful harvest made the difference between life and death. Without a good harvest they were destined to starve!

There were no supermarkets. There was no one other than the Native Americans to borrow, buy or beg food from. Although the Native Americans had been helpful, survival for the Pilgrims rested on their own efforts. What they harvested meant life or death to everyone in the colony.

Harvest festivals or thanksgiving celebrations had been a common practice in many parts of the world for centuries, ever since the beginnings of agriculture some 8000 years ago. Berkeley Plantation in Virginia lays claim to the first Thanksgiving in what is now the United States, two years earlier. Most people, however, give credit to the Pilgrims for the beginning of our Thanksgiving tradition.

In 1789, following a proclamation by President George Washington, America celebrated its first day of thanksgiving under its new constitution. This was not a decree for an annual holiday but was to give thanks for the new constitution that had just been adopted. During the following years, in our country's history, Thanksgiving was observed in some states and in some communities but was not recognized as a national day of Thanksgiving until signed into law by Abraham Lincoln in 1863. Lincoln decreed the last Thursday in November as a national holiday. In 1941, the United States Congress permanently established the fourth Thursday of each November as a national holiday.

A turkey dinner for Thanksgiving dates back to the Pilgrims. Both deer and turkey meat was consumed at their first Thanksgiving. A whole turkey at the Thanksgiving dinner table serves as a more appropriate and readily available symbol of this early Thanksgiving than a deer and has become a tradition for the majority of America's families.

The National Turkey Federation, starting in 1947, has presented the President of the United States with a turkey just prior to Thanksgiving. For publicity purposes, the live turkey presented has been granted a pardon by the President and is retired to live out its life at a special wildlife sanctuary. In addition to the live turkey, a dressed, ready-for-the-oven turkey is given to the President. This turkey is beyond the President's capabilities to pardon and I am suspicious it provides the central portion of a delectable turkey dinner.

The consumption of turkey is far greater per capita in the United States than almost all other countries. The pounds of turkey eaten in November surpasses by far the consumption of turkey in any of the other eleven months. As a turkey farmer I gave thanks to the Pilgrims for starting this tradition and to Abraham Lincoln for making Thanksgiving an annual national holiday.

# Processing and Marketing Turkeys
## in the 1930s and 40s

The changes in food and food handling, during the last 80 years, are truly amazing. What I describe here was common practice with turkeys. Comparative changes have occurred with other food products. Today, however, practices we used 80 and more years ago, are still common throughout the developing world.

The 1930s and early 1940s were still the era of the small farm and small business. It required thousands of small businesses or farms to produce the equivalent of what one large corporation does today. Normally each small farm produced several products, as a form of insurance, against disaster, should weather or disease destroy one of them. In agriculture, large corporate farms producing huge quantities of one or several agricultural products were unknown.

Our farm had a dairy, a variety of field crops and turkeys. We were one of many thousands of small farms across the United States that had a flock of turkeys. Some farms sold their live turkeys to dealers or retail food stores that slaughtered the turkeys for their customers. Others sold live turkeys directly to the consumer who slaughtered and processed them at home. Still others, including ourselves, slaughtered and marketed their turkeys directly to stores and to the retail customer. During this period of time, there was no inspection service and no rules and regulations regarding the processing and handling of poultry. Every farmer had his own methods of processing with only two requirements, satisfaction of the customer and hopefully a profit.

Our turkey processing facility was a tobacco stripping room in the middle of a tobacco shed, constructed in 1900, for hanging stalks of tobacco to dry. From February to November, when the room wasn't being used for either turkeys or tobacco, it was the farm shop. Other turkey farms may have used a woodshed, a machinery storage building or a branch of a tree for their processing facility. Running water and metal surfaces that could be easily cleaned, were unheard of on the farm.

Inserting a narrow knife, deep into the bird's mouth, and cutting the arteries in its neck was the normal method to kill the turkeys. Next, the turkeys were usually dry picked, since this required no special equipment. There are hundreds of feathers on a turkey, making it a great deal of work to pull the dry feathers by hand, especially since pliers were needed to pull some of the larger feathers. Once the feathers were removed, the turkey was ready to be sold. The turkeys, marketed in this form, were called NY dressed, regardless of which part of the country they were processed and sold. The housewife removed the head, feet and internal parts prior to preparation for roasting.

Since no farm had refrigeration to cool the turkeys at this time, almost all turkeys were marketed NY dressed. NY dressed turkeys had a much longer shelf life than a turkey processed ready for the oven.

Mother Nature designed the turkey to produce its young during the spring of the year. Man had not yet manipulated nature's timetable, in the 1930s, so turkeys were not normally large enough for marketing until November. By this time the outside temperature was lower and a NY dressed turkey could go without refrigeration for several days.

The NY dressed turkeys were normally marketed with a small parchment bag tied around their head, so any remaining blood in the bird would not soak through the brown grocery bag it which it was marketed. Even the US government, during World War II, bought NY dressed turkeys packed in large barrels and then frozen, to feed its servicemen. The army cooks had a disagreeable job, thawing the barrels full of turkeys and then removing all the extraneous internal and external parts, before preparing the birds for roasting.

Processing turkeys on our farm was somewhat different, but comparing the process with today's standards, I marvel at our success even though we were using the accepted procedures of the time. Our farm was one of a few that used a hard scald to loosen the feathers after slaughter. There is no fat underneath the skin on a turkey leg and since the skin is very tender, we dry picked the legs before scalding. If we had not done this there would have been dark blotches all over the legs where the skin cuticle had been damaged during picking. After the legs were picked, the turkey was scalded by dipping it in a vat of water at a temperature of 200+ degrees. This temperature loosened the feathers and set the layer of fat under the skin, allowing relatively easy removal of the remaining feathers without damaging the skin. After picking, a washcloth and water were used to clean the skin of any of the gelatin-like substance, from an immature feather, left on the skin. The washcloth was a quarter of a cotton feed bag that had been cut for this purpose and had never seen water prior to washing the turkeys!

After picking, the turkey was dipped in another vat of 200+degree water for "plumping". This temperature had a shrinking effect upon the skin, supposedly making the turkey look meatier. In retrospect, although we did not recognize it at the time, many of the bacteria on the skin were killed by the hot water.

After the "plumping", the turkey was tossed into a galvanized tank of cool water for about an hour. Next it was hung from a nail with string around its feet, to cool toward whatever might be the temperature of the outside air. The air temperature could be anything from 0 to 70 degrees, depending upon the weather that day. Normally each turkey was moved to market the same day it was killed or on the following morning. If the overnight air temperature was below freezing, dressed turkeys, held over night, were moved to the basement of our house to keep them from freezing.

Prior to the turkeys being sold, a parchment bag was tied around the head and a large red tag, stating the name, address and phone number for our farm, was tied to one leg. Each tag carried the statement, printed in large words, "If satisfied tell others, if not tell us." The turkeys were then weighed, several at a time, on steelyard scales, a type of balance scale used throughout the world for several thousand years. After weighing they were individually bagged, piled on a stake rack truck, covered with a canvas and transported to the various stores that had ordered them.

Since starting to grow turkeys in 1923, our farm had gradually built a retail business with customers coming directly to the farm or having a turkey delivered directly to their home. We also went to the Syracuse public market where customers could purchase one of our turkeys. To satisfy this retail clientele, additional processing was necessary. It included removing the feet, head, crop and intestines. The housewife still had to remove the lungs, heart, liver and gizzard as well as remove the stones, feed and trash that was in the gizzard.

The methods I have described seem extremely crude but I never heard of one of our turkeys spoiling or anyone getting sick. Perhaps it was because people were more resistant to bacteria, at that time, because of their continual exposure.

With the end of World War II, there were many changes in the US, including changes on farms. Farms became larger, government requirements increased and specialization of production became the norm. Over the next 30 years almost all of the small independent turkey farms gradually disappeared. Large integrated agricultural corporations appeared and contracted with farmers to grow live turkeys for them. Most of the farmers didn't own the turkeys they grew, but received something for each bird grown. A few independent turkey growers were able to survive, but to survive they needed to develop niche markets. The costs of production were greater for the small independent making it impossible to compete on price alone. Our farm took steps to produce the best turkey possible and through gradual expansion, innovation and cost control, continued to prosper.

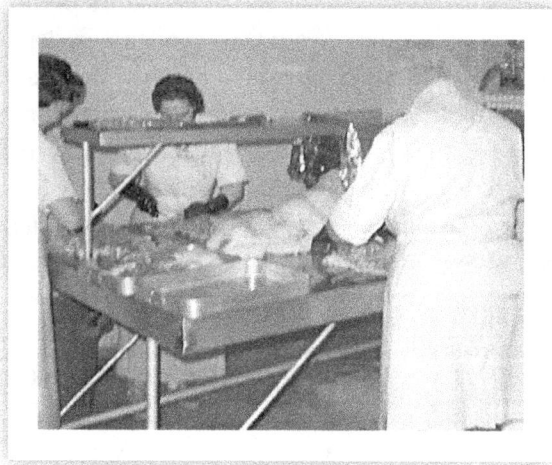

*Circa 1964. Connie Smith, Rose Dodge and Ida Roth are boning and then trimming turkey meat to form turkey rolls. The meat was seasoned, wrapped in aluminum foil and then cooked very slowly in an oven.*

# Sleeping with the Turkeys

Hundreds of live turkeys, in a field surrounded by a five-foot wire fence, attracted a variety of hungry predators fully as much as stacks of candy would attract young boys. All of that fresh meat walking, running and flying around in the field most certainly would have made the mouths of fox, owl and a hungry man salivate. Our goal was to turn the turkeys into dollars that provided for the needs of our family. We violently objected to predators coming into the field to take turkeys under the, "eat now, never pay policy."

Recognizing that we could not be successful growing turkeys with this free lunch policy, we took steps towards a pay only program. We fitted a small movable building with a bed and parked it in the middle of our turkey field. Each evening as darkness crept in, my dad or one of his helpers with flashlight and shotgun in hand, headed to the turkey field to spend the night. There was also a dog, fastened with a chain and furnished with a doghouse in the field. The dog barked when a fox came near the turkeys, awakening the person on duty. This activity would send the fox on its way to search elsewhere for its gastronomic delights.

Owls, which thoroughly enjoyed our tender young turkeys, had to be handled differently. A long cedar pole was set vertically in the ground to provide the owl with a perch as he surveyed the field for the perfect lunch. What the owl didn't know was that there was a trap on the top of the pole!

As an eight-year old boy, I thought it must be a lot of fun heading out in the evening to sleep with the turkeys. I begged my dad to let me go with him and he finally agreed. I felt I was pretty big stuff heading out into the night with my dad and his shotgun in hand. I had visions of the thieves we would catch and of saving turkeys from a hungry fox.

The anticipated joy soon disappeared. He put the shotgun on the wall and we climbed into the one existing bed. No money had been squandered on good springs or a comfortable mattress. The bed, mattress and springs probably came out of the attic, having been shunted there 20 years earlier. My dad's 200 pounds made the springs and mattress settle in the middle. When he lay down he almost disappeared. I tried to sleep, without rolling down and disturbing him, but had to hang on to the edge of the bed to keep from rolling down what seemed like a steep mountain side. It was a long night!

After what seemed hours, I drifted asleep to be prematurely awakened by the alarm clock jangling at 5:00 in the morning. It was time to get up and go to work! There had been no marauding foxes, no light-fingered-homo sapiens, not even an owl on top of the pole. My hope for excitement had vanished. Never again did I ask my dad if I could sleep with the turkeys!

*Circa 1938. This is a flock of turkeys on pasture. Note the sleeping shanty in the upper right where a man slept at night to guard the turkeys from predators. At this time we grew both white and bronze turkeys.*

# The Turkey, A Flying Machine

L ooking into the bin of plump round turkeys at the supermarket, shaped almost like basketballs, you would have similar thoughts to the audience watching the Wright brothers at Kitty Hawk, "there is a bird that could never fly!" The turkey in the bin didn't always look like it does now. Seventy years ago it had long legs, big wings and could fly.

Nature designed the turkey to be a running and flying machine! Instead of wheels, like an airplane, the long legs could move it rapidly over the ground and then with a few hearty wing strokes be soaring into a high tree or across the field. This ability was splendid for a turkey in the wild but when the turkey was domesticated the turkey farmer received many frustrations.

It was necessary to have a five-foot fence around turkeys put in fields of pasture, however, each day a number of turkeys flew over the fence. No, they weren't searching for freedom because as soon as they were over the fence they walked back and forth, along a few feet of fence, trying to get back into the pasture. Would they ever consider flying back in? Never! The turkey farmer had to open a gate and drive them back inside. Once inside they would immediately fly to join the others inside the fence, as if they had been gone for a month.

When fall arrived with its cold rains and snow, the turkeys' lives on pasture were not as pleasant. As Thanksgiving approached the weather gradually became worse while the turkeys' days became numbered. It was time to move them to a field near the processing plant. Turkeys will herd together into groups like cattle and can be driven some distance when they are willing to cooperate.

Quite often, on a Saturday morning when there was no school, dad would delegate my sister and I, along with some neighboring children, to help him drive the turkeys closer to the processing plant. He chose morning because that was the time turkeys normally foraged for food, whereas later in the day they would be thinking of roosting for the night and wouldn't be as willing to leave their home.

We all had light sticks, four or five feet long, with one in each hand as an extension of our arms. This was to make the turkeys think they couldn't run between us back to their old pasture. We rounded up a few hundred turkeys and started the drive. Things would go quite well until we were almost out of sight of their old home and all of a sudden two or three turkeys ran between two of us. If they were successful all the others would follow; some running and the rest flying, well over our heads, back home.

We then had to start the turkey drive over again, trying to be extremely vigilant so none would sneak by us again. Often they flew back a second or third time before we were successful. It became a question as to who would win, the turkeys or the humans. It was very frustrating to be outsmarted by a flock of turkeys. Do you suppose the turkeys had sent out a spy that reported back telling them that we were taking them to the processing plant?

*Circa 1980. This picture is driving turkeys from one of the growing buildings to the processing plant. Driving two flocks of 200 to 300 was easier than driving one flock of 500 for both the turkeys and the drivers. The second flock had a tendency to follow the first flock without much coaxing. In later years we drove the turkeys onto specially made trailers and then they had a short ride to the processing plant.*

# Turkey Love

Yes, even turkeys enjoy making love! The expression, 'love makes the world go around' also applies to turkeys. Let me tell you about turkey love.

Ever since the turkey first evolved, when spring arrives, thoughts of love fill the minds of both the hen and the tom turkey. The hen starts building a well-hidden nest from last year's dried grasses, which are found close by. She spends several days gathering pieces of grass and forming them into the shape of a shallow basket to provide insulation under and at the sides for the eggs.

We must not overlook her lover: tom, the turkey gobbler. He spreads his feathers, looking as big and beautiful as possible, once the first signs of spring appear. He struts, in front of all the hens in his domain, trying to impress each of them as to his worthiness as a lover. The hen ignores the strutting turkey gobbler until her nest is ready. Now her romantic instincts surface as she sits on the ground enticing the strutting gobbler to be her lover. A few romantic moments later, all the essentials have been achieved toward her path to motherhood!

Until the eggs are all laid, the turkey hen goes about her usual business of eating bugs, grasshoppers, and whatever seeds she can find. She stops at the nest daily but only long enough to lay another egg and turn the ones laid earlier. She is very clever, stopping laying prior to having more eggs than she can cover with her body, about 15. She doesn't set on them until she is through laying to ensure that all of the eggs hatch on the same day.

Numerous yolks started growing in the hen prior to her romantic rendezvous with tom. They were of varying size allowing one egg to be ready for fertilization each day. As the yolk traveled down the oviduct, the albumen was added, followed by a tough membrane and finally it was all encompassed in a shell. Just prior to the egg slipping out of her oviduct, the hen placed dozens of small brown dots on the egg, guaranteeing to all observers that it is a genuine turkey egg.

When the last egg is laid, the hen has four weeks of steady work, keeping the eggs warm and turning them in the nest several times a day. The turning allows the embryo to continually remain in the center of the egg without adhering to the side. She can only leave the nest for short periods or the eggs will cool below 100 degrees and may not hatch. Mr. Turkey Gobbler has gone on his way, looking for other candidates for motherhood, as quickly as he has satisfied the hen's romantic desires. He has no desire to set on a nest when other far more tempting opportunities await him.

Day and night for 28 days the turkey hen sets on her eggs waiting for the stork to arrive with perhaps 8, 10, or as many as 12 baby poults. With only a few minutes away from the nest several times a day she anxiously awaits motherhood.

Finally, the hen turkey hears weak pecking sounds under her. It is the baby poults pecking circular holes in the upper part of the eggs. They now push their way out into the warm world under mother hen's feathers. Nature has provided a very hard end on the beak of the poult to help it pick through the shell. An air space has also been provided inside the upper part of the egg for each new arrival.

When most of the eggs have hatched, the hen leaves the nest to look for bugs and tender grass. The baby poults follow closely behind, instinctively finding and eating from the same menu as mama. They don't need to find much food the first few days as 'mother nature' has arranged for the poults to develop from the white of the egg leaving the yoke, remaining inside each poult's abdomen, to serve as a supplemental food source.

Within a relatively short time the hen heads back to the nest, followed by the poults who snuggle under her feathers. They may find a new brother or sister waiting for them that has been a bit tardy coming out of the egg. Each day the foraging excursions become longer until in a few days mom's nest and warm feathers are only needed at night or when the weather is cold and rainy

The poults follow the mother hen for several months. They stay together as a group through the winter. As spring starts to appear, romantic thoughts come to both mother hen and her poults, now fully mature. Each heads in a different direction, searching for love.

# Evolution of Turkey Products

Until the 1940's Thanksgiving and Christmas were about the only times turkey was consumed. Until that time turkeys were usually sold alive to be prepared by either the housewife or the butcher. Dressing the live turkeys in preparation for the dinner table was not a task that most butchers or consumers enjoyed. In 1923, Plainville Turkey Farm started growing turkeys and solved the problem for the butcher and consumer by slaughtering the bird and removing the feathers. By the 1940's, Plainville Turkey Farm was producing turkeys that were nearly ready for the housewife to put in the oven.

When the Central NY Regional Market opened, on the northern edge of Syracuse in 1938, one of the buildings at the market was a poultry dressing plant. Farmers from a wide area of Central and Northern NY brought their live poultry to the market, which was purchased by both the housewife and the storekeeper. They carried their live purchases to the processing plant and for a reasonable fee it was quickly bled, feathers removed and becoming NY Dressed, in a very short time. There had been public markets in Syracuse since 1835 but they had been located in the central part of the city near butchers who slaughtered the birds.

After World War II refrigeration and freezers became common, permitting turkeys to be frozen and available anytime of the year. The annual consumption of turkey gradually increased from about 4 pounds per person in the 1940's to approximately 19 pounds today.

Almost all turkeys produced in the United States are broad breasted whites. These birds were derived from the broad breasted bronze but selected for white feathers. Immature bronze feathers often left undesirable dark spots, from the pigment of immature feathers, under the skin of the market ready bird.

At Plainville, we moved turkey processing several steps forward in 1958. As I approached potential customers to purchase large tom turkeys, I found that they were looking for turkey that was convenient for them to prepare and serve. I heard of a Cooperative Extension agent on Long Island who had demonstrated turkey boning to turkey growers on the Island. I drove there to see him bone a turkey and came back to Plainville where I duplicated the process.

Some potential customers wanted a product that was fully cooked and others wanted a boneless product that was ready for roasting. After much experimentation I was able to provide both types of product for the customers. We were traveling in unknown waters, as there were almost none of these products available on the market.

The first convenient cooked product to come on the market was a turkey roll. They were generally of poor quality and before long had created a bad name for turkey rolls. Our turkey roll was roasted and of high quality. When selling these rolls to restaurants and supermarkets I carried some napkins and a knife, providing the customer with the opportunity to make an educated decision. Amazingly, I obtained a new customer on over half of my sales calls.

When entering a new field of endeavor unknown challenges usually appear. My customers wanted only the breast of the turkey leaving us with surplus wings, drumsticks, thighs, giblets and necks. Bob Baker, a poultry professor at Cornell, helped me turn some of these surplus items into bologna-type products but their sale never took off. We ran successful specials on drumsticks and thighs with stores but most of the necks and giblets ended up going to mink farmers.

Over the years we produced a great variety of turkey products. Seasonings can be added to turkey to produce products that initially would not seem possible. There will undoubtedly be many new turkey products produced in the future but most of us, when we think of turkey, will remember the turkey with its wonderful aroma and delicious flavor that we enjoyed at our family Thanksgiving feast!

# Mothering Baby Turkeys

I have been a mother to thousands! A mother to baby turkeys! The correct name for baby turkeys is "poults", and back in the 1930s and 1940s poults took a great deal of mothering.

Eggs put into an incubator, four weeks later, turned into cute little balls of down filled with energy. They arrived at the farm within 24 hours of escaping from the egg and had no mother hen to show them the ways of life, so I became their substitute mother.

A small wooden building, called a brooder house, approximately 12 by 14 feet, had been thoroughly cleaned and disinfected for the poults. This was to ensure that they had a hospital clean environment to begin their life. The floor was covered with a layer of dried sugar cane and a stove was lighted and regulated to provide a temperature of 95 degrees around its base, duplicating the temperature under mother turkey's feathers. Several waterers and feeders were placed around the base of the stove and a small woven wire fence encircled it all, to eliminate any possibility of the poults wandering into one of the corners of the building and getting cold.

After all of this preparation, 200 baby poults were placed in the pen. Immediately the poults started exploring their pen and saying peep, peep, peep. My goal was to have them find the feed and water as quickly as possible. This was their first opportunity to experience eating and drinking. With one flock of poults I had even dipped each poult's beak in a waterer with the hope that each would remember where to go for another drink. I even placed brightly colored marbles in the feeders with the hope that the marbles would attract the turkeys to the feed. After trying both, I quickly decided that they were wasted effort.

The new poults had to be watched very closely the first day because if they felt a draft, they huddled together with the ones in the center getting smothered. We had about 15 similar small buildings so I kept busy moving from one building to another checking the poults, until darkness came and they settled down for the night.

The buildings were heated, each by an oil (kerosene) stove with a six-gallon oil container in each building, which needed to be filled daily. When it was windy, even in the middle of the night, it was necessary to check the stoves regularly because a strong gust of wind could blow out their fires. With no heat coming from the stove, the poults crowded together for warmth and smothered the ones in the middle.

When the poults were a week old it was necessary to remove the wire fence because they had begun to fly. When they were two weeks old we placed a sun porch (a wooden cage on legs with wire on three sides plus top and bottom) with the open side next to the brooder house. There was a small vertical sliding door, which opened into the sun porch in that side of the brooder house. We opened this door each morning to allow the poults to come out on the sun porch. The wire on the bottom was sufficiently heavy to support the turkeys, and allow their droppings to fall through the wire underneath. Water and feed were both placed on the sun porch to encourage the turkeys to spend their time outside.

Each evening we drove the poults into the brooder house so they wouldn't get cold during the night and also to protect them from a rainstorm. Yelling or pounding a stick on the top of the sun porch helped encourage them to go inside the brooder house. You can imagine how difficult it could be on a warm summer night. I often had to crawl into their sun porch and push them inside. It always took two people, as one person had to wait inside to quickly close the door before they started coming back out.

Finally, at eight weeks of age, the turkeys (they are big enough now so we call them turkeys instead of poults) were large enough to be transferred to a turkey range (a fenced field of grass with roosts, feeders and waterers) to spend their next four months. Two people working together drove about a dozen turkeys into one corner of the brooder house and caught them by both legs so as not to hurt them. Each person carried about six turkeys because they only weighed about three pounds each. They were put in cages for transportation to the range. At the range we reached into the cages and lifted each turkey, one after another, out of the cage and let it fly to the ground.

Fortunately my mothering of the poults lasted only eight weeks rather than the five years it takes for a mother to prepare her child for kindergarten. Additionally, I didn't have to change any diapers. After they were moved to range, however, I had to clean up the entire eight weeks of their deposits.

# Nature's Fury

When the weather is beautiful, there is no better place for turkeys than on a lush pasture. By not being confined to a building, they are free to fly, run, eat the grass and enjoy the bugs that are a part of nature's outdoors. Unfortunately nature doesn't always cooperate and a pleasant day can quickly become violent.

The weather in central New York is more unpredictable than in many areas of the country because of the presence of Lake Ontario to the north. The prevailing winds come from the northwest, diagonally across the lake. A sunny day north of the lake is very often a stormy day, on our farm, south of the lake.

We never put young turkeys on pasture before the latter part of May, after the threat of a late snowstorm had passed. Usually the weather is pleasant in June, July and August but a sudden thunderstorm with hail can be disastrous.

In the summer of 1954, there was a hailstorm with very high winds and large hailstones. We had a flock of 12-week old turkeys on pasture that got pelted with the hailstones. Several of the turkeys, that now weighed about six pounds, received broken legs and broken wings from the force of the hail. I didn't have them fill out a questionnaire but I am sure there were also a lot of sore heads and backs. The hailstorm was so bad that over the next week we replaced over 100 broken windows in the farm buildings.

Because we had no large growing buildings for our turkeys until 1954, the turkeys we grew for the Christmas market had to remain outside until they were processed. In addition, there were always surplus birds remaining after Christmas that had to stay on the pasture, which was now a field covered with snow, until we were able to market them. Sometimes this was as late as March. The Syracuse area, where our farm is located, receives an average of 110 inches of snow each winter.

Because turkeys are native to the area, they can sustain cold weather and snow very well. We provided roosts for the turkeys that were three feet above the ground, which worked well during the average snowstorm. Occasionally we received several feet of snow, with a wind blowing it into drifts five or six feet high during the night. When checking the turkeys the following morning anyone would think the turkeys had disappeared. They did disappear, under the snow! We used large scoop shovels to carefully remove the snow covering the turkeys. Fortunately air can move through light snow. Between the insulation provided by the turkeys' feathers and the insulation from the snow, the turkeys survived very well. The covering over the turkeys was as soft as down from a goose but even so, I don't believe I would enjoy being buried under snow all night!

*Circa 1950. Turkeys outside, in the wintertime, on what had previously been pasture. It was a difficult life for them. Notice the white turkey in the foreground, standing on one leg. Yes, if they weren't on the roosts their feet got cold. There was very little shelter for them.*

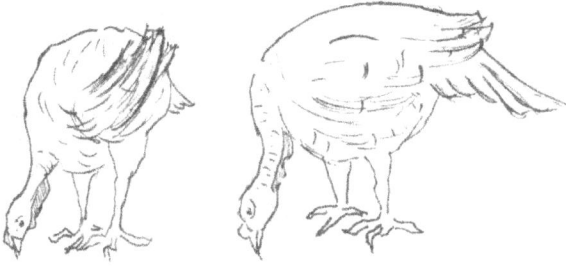

# World War II and Turkeys

With the advent of war on December 7, 1941, our United States peacetime economy shifted from low gear to overdrive in a wartime economy. We needed to place an all out effort toward winning the war, while giving up some of our normal peacetime practices. Eventually we experienced gas rationing, tire rationing, shoe rationing and meat rationing. The government also created the Office of Price Administration (OPA) establishing the maximum price that could be charged for a product.

Poultry was not rationed but maximum prices were established for all categories, both wholesale and retail, for live, NY dressed (only feathers and blood removed), and eviscerated. Until this time we sold our turkeys, both NY dressed and eviscerated. The maximum price was more favorable for eviscerated so NY dressed became part of the past. Red meat not only had maximum prices but was also rationed with a family receiving a specific number of meat stamps for each member. This rationing increased the demand for poultry, including our turkeys.

As Thanksgiving neared we began to receive calls from meat markets we had never done business with. We told them we had no extra turkeys because we would continue to sell to our previous customers. Some of them said, "We'll pay you more." When we reminded them that selling the turkeys for more than the price established by the government was illegal, they replied, "You can invoice us for that price but we'll slip you the extra money under the table." My dad refused to do this.

Our farm is out in the country and we even had to put a sign at the end of the driveway stating that we had no turkeys except for our regular customers. We had taken dressed turkeys to the Central NY Regional Market at Syracuse for many years and didn't want to let those customers down. The big problem was we knew only a few of the retail customers that had purchased our turkeys in previous years. We decided to take turkeys to the market, maintaining our presence and supplying some of our previous customers while gaining new ones.

Arrangements were made with the market staff to weigh the turkeys in the wee hours of the morning before the market opened so as to be ready to sell at 6:00 a.m. when the lights came on and the market opened. (All poultry was required to be weighed on the market's scales.) When the market opened, the market management required the customers to line up and take their turn. We limited each customer to one turkey and sold the turkeys as fast as we could make change. Our 250 fresh turkeys were all sold within an hour, whereas it would have normally taken at least six hours. Each person was happy to have a turkey and was not particular about looks or size.

Government regulations created a major blimp in the law of supply and demand. We, like most Americans, were willing to cooperate and do all we could to bring a quick and successful conclusion to the war.

*Circa 1948. This shows Plainville turkeys being sold on the CNY Regional Market at Syracuse. The turkeys are displayed on top of tobacco boxes and have no covering over them. Additional turkeys to be sold are in white paper bags on the back of the truck. The author took the picture of Glen Bratt on the left and Harold Meaker on the right ,who had just beckoned to the unknown person in the center to join them in the picture.*

# Schoolchildren Visits

About 1950, school children began visiting the farm by the busload. Turkey farms were not very common and apparently teachers felt a visit to the local turkey farm was a worthwhile learning experience. Perhaps the turkey's position as the centerpiece of America's Thanksgiving also helped create interest.

Initially, there was no planning for our visitors. We took the children to a pasture full of turkeys, let them pet one and answered their questions such as, "What do the turkeys eat?" "How do you tell a boy turkey from a girl turkey?" We gave each child two feathers and the children would leave the farm a bit wiser and perhaps with a little remembrance of their walk in the turkey field on the bottoms of their shoes.

In 1953, I married a young schoolteacher named Janice, who loved children and took over the schoolchildren's visits to the turkey farm. She wanted each child to have a rich learning experience when visiting the farm, so she expanded the tour. Now the children were able to walk into the processing plant and see the turkeys being prepared for market. Today, parents would shudder at having their little kindergartener see something like that but 50 years ago people living in the country thought nothing of it. My wife showed the children a turkey's gizzard, which is full of little stones that grind the turkeys' food, and explained many facts about turkeys. She also sent each child home with an apple, two feathers and a pencil. We felt that a pencil, with a little advertising on it, might remind the parents about our turkey farm at an appropriate time in the future.

Apparently, positive reports about the schoolchildren's visits to the Plainville Turkey Farm reached teachers in distant school districts, as the number of schools sending busloads of children to the farm continued to grow. The visit to the turkey farm was changing as American society became further removed from farm life. A stop at the processing plant was no longer acceptable to the parents of some of the children.

We decided that it was time to polish our public relations and constructed a combination retail store and visitor center. We introduced a variety of farm animals to the school children and other visitors, including a cow, horse, pigs, sheep, goats and of course turkeys. The children learned about these farm animals and had the opportunity to pet them. We also had an animated turkey named Professor Plainville conversing with animated Farmer Pete, who was sitting on an old tractor. The verbal exchanges between these two characters provided an enjoyable learning experience for the children.

The visit to the farm was a positive learning experience for thousands of young children. Over the years I have talked with or met a number of adults, from several different states, that have told me how much they enjoyed their visit to the Plainville Turkey Farm as schoolchildren.

We can't take credit for everything they learned, however. One teacher reported the response of a little boy, when she asked her class, "Where was the first Thanksgiving?" He forcibly responded, "At the Plainville Turkey Farm!"

*Circa 1954. Janice Bitz, on the left, brought her kindergarden class to the farm to see the turkeys. The next year, after leaving the paid teaching field, and for the next 20 years she gave turkey tours to many thousands of schoolchildren through-out Central New York.*

# Fires on the Turkey Farm

The mother turkey, called a hen, has a body temperature of over 100 degrees and sits on her eggs four weeks before they hatch. After hatching, the baby turkeys, called poults, stay under the hen's body feathers at night and also during the daytime, when they aren't out scavenging for food with their mother.

When man decided to substitute an incubator and a brooder house for the hen, it was necessary to duplicate the temperatures needed for incubation and brooding. Because of this, we had numerous brooder stoves with a live flame, to keep the baby poults warm.

The stoves used on our farm, until the 1950s, burned kerosene. Things went smoothly as long as nothing malfunctioned but the stoves needed to be closely watched. The brooder houses were not insulated and the stoves needed to produce a great deal of heat on a cold windy night. Dried sugar cane, which we put on the floors for litter helped prevent fires because the sugar cane smoldered for some time before breaking out in flames. We had more than one brooder house with an area of charred floorboards where we stopped a fire before it was too late.

We had some fine neighbors, one of whom was a farmer who lived a half-mile away and grew some chickens. One night he happened to look out of a window in his house at 1:00 a.m. and saw what appeared to be a serious fire on our farm. He jumped in his truck and drove up our driveway, past the house, to where the brooder houses were located. He saw that one was almost completely destroyed by a fire. The brooder houses were placed about 50 feet apart, to prevent a potential fire from spreading to other brooder houses. The next day, about 7:00 a.m., my dad's phone rang and when he answered, the neighbor asked, "Are you missing anything this morning?" My dad responded that a brooder house with turkeys had burned during the night and asked how the neighbor knew. He stated, "I noticed a fire at your farm and drove over to help you. The building was almost completely burned and since was no danger to the other buildings I decided to let you get a good night's sleep."

By 1990, our turkey production and our brooding buildings were much larger. Methods of brooding had changed and we were heating with propane gas. One evening a gas stove malfunctioned in a 50 foot by 350 foot building containing over 5,000 young turkeys. The fire started near one end of the building. Fortunately a neighbor saw the fire before it had spread to the whole building. About a dozen fire trucks quickly arrived and were able to save a little over half of the building. There were no turkeys in the portion they saved but the 5,000 poults in the end with the fire were killed by heat or suffocation from smoke inhalation.

The destroyed building was needed for poults scheduled to arrive in three weeks. At 6:00 a.m. the next day my son had both a building contractor and the insurance adjustor at the site. Demolition of the ruins and new construction started immediately. I am proud to say that a new building was ready for use when the poults arrived.

*Circa 1953. Robert Bitz is in the farm's first refrigerated facility, a freezer. These are large tom turkeys that were put in plastic bags and covered with a cotton netting so they could be stacked. There are also turkeys in the used wooden chicken boxes on each side. These were surplus turkeys that were stored to be sold to restaurants during the winter and spring months before the farm's venture into further processing a few years later.*

# False Teeth for Turkeys

The poor turkey has no teeth! Turkeys are foragers, eating grass, seeds, worms and a multitude of other items provided by nature. Our domestic turkeys were fed whole grains; oats, wheat and corn. These feeds are hard and cannot be digested unless they are ground into fine particles. Somehow this coarse food must be ground into small particles for the turkey to grow and, believe it or not, the turkey uses false teeth to accomplish this task.

In every turkey there is an organ called a gizzard. The gizzard, in a mature turkey, is about the size of a billiard ball. The gizzard is the largest of three edible organs; heart, liver and gizzard, found in a ready-to-cook turkey. The gizzard is a solid dense meat with a small sac, a little larger than a golf ball, inside. Inside this sac are the turkey's false teeth, which grind the grain the turkey has eaten into fine particles. The false teeth are actually small stones, about the size of a kernel of corn. In the ready-to-cook turkey the gizzard has been opened at the processing plant, to remove the sac with its small stones (false teeth).

When the turkey swallows its food, the food passes directly to a storage area called the "crop". The crop holds all the food a turkey needs from morning until night. The food moves, little by little, from the crop into the turkey's gizzard. Muscular contractions of the gizzard press the stones together, again and again, gradually grinding the grain into small particles.

Turkeys swallow small stones as needed, which move to the gizzard to do the work of grinding. These small stones gradually become smaller as they rub against the grain and each other. When they become too small to grind effectively they pass through the intestine and are discharged with food waste.

On our turkey farm, the turkeys' false teeth were granite stones, shipped by railroad car from North Carolina. We purchased four sizes of stones, which are actually called grit rather than false teeth, increasing the size of the stones as the turkeys grew. The smallest were about the size of breadcrumbs and the largest about the size of an eraser on a pencil. The grit was crushed, at the North Carolina plant, from large granite boulders and then screened to obtain the proper sizes. It was important to use a hard stone that could withstand the constant grinding and not be dissolved by the digestive juices in the turkeys' intestinal tract. In recent years turkey farmers have ground grain in feed mills, before feeding it to their turkeys, eliminating the need to furnish their turkeys with false teeth

We had a special 'false teeth' feeder for the turkeys. They seemed to know when their old ones needed replacing. Allowing a pound of grit for each turkey during its growing period required a ton of grit for each 2,000 turkeys. Since we grew many thousands of turkeys each year, we provided our clients with more false teeth than all of the dentists in New York State!

*Circa 1950. Harry Bitz, father of Robert Bitz and one of the founders of Plainville Turkey Farm, is holding two New York dressed tom turkeys that weigh over 30 pounds each. The end user, a butcher or restaurant, removed the head, feet and internal organs before roasting the turkeys.*

# Garden Fertilizer

Turkeys eat a high protein diet that provides a waste product higher in nitrogen than other farm animals. The high level of nitrogen makes plants grow rapidly and gives them a healthy look when the proper amount is applied.

Each year we used turkey manure to fertilize our corn and knowing how much to apply we always had an excellent crop yield. In the 1950s, I thought that there might be a market for some of that good fertilizer by selling it to homeowners through lawn and garden stores. This was well before people were thinking organic and prior to the appearance of the great variety of fertilizers that are available today. We had a large turkey growing building, with a concrete floor, in which we had housed turkeys during the winter. The manure in this building was very dry so I hired a man with a large portable feed grinder to come to the farm and grind the manure. The large grinder did a good job so that even the turkey feathers were not recognizable.

We put 25 pounds of manure in each of 200 plastic bags. I developed instructions for its use and also a questionnaire to place in each bag. Next I went to several lawn and garden stores, leaving a few bags at each store, for the store to give to some of its customers. This was a case of 'putting the cart before the horse' as I had done no previous testing of the product to see how well it performed. I found that the stores were willing to give the product away but that no one was willing to pay for it. We ended up dumping the contents of most of the remaining bags on our cornfields.

In retrospect, I am fortunate the product didn't sell, as it had not been through a composting cycle. If it got wet, it became its original smelly turkey manure. The odor of turkey manure on the farm is a normal part of country life but smelly turkey manure, on a suburbanite's flowerbed, could have more than minor consequences.

Another experience with this by-product of turkey production was with neighbors who grew vegetables on gravel soil that was not very productive. They asked if they could have some of our turkey manure. We responded, "Certainly, help yourself and take all you would like." Summer passed and in the early fall we asked them if the turkey manure provided them with a good vegetable crop. They embarrassedly responded that they had applied too much of the free turkey manure. Shortly after a vegetable started to grow, it died or was stunted and produced nothing. Excessive use of the manure had burned their vegetables. The next year they applied no manure and had a good garden. This was another verification of the old saying, 'too much of a good thing can be dangerous'. It is especially appropriate when the item is free!

*Circa 1938. Plainville Turkey Farm had neither a tractor nor a combine so this man was hired to combine the grain. In the background is a row of 12 X14 foot brooder houses with attached sun porches. Much of the material for the brooder houses came from wooden tobacco boxes. Notice the stovepipe stacks extending from the center of each brooder house to provide exhaust from the oil fired brooder stoves.*

# Proof of Murphy's Law

We had just constructed our first large turkey building. It was an 8,000 square foot state of the art (for 1954), brooding building (growing turkeys from day old to eight weeks) and we were very proud of it. All of our previous brooding buildings had each been less than 200 square feet, were drafty and required a great amount of labor. We had obtained plans from Cornell University, talked with one of their agricultural engineers concerning the best construction methods and carefully built it, with mostly our own labor.

At that time, pressure treated lumber was not readily available so we found a grove of locust trees, which are highly resistant to rot, to use for poles. We peeled the bark from the poles, dug holes in the ground, placed the poles and started construction in early February. During the winter our workload was relatively light and by the end of May we had completed the building, installed new brooder stoves, automatic waterers and even a new automatic feeder. It was spanking clean and ready for the 4,000 day-old turkeys (poults) that were scheduled to arrive in early June.

In the early 1950s, we started two flocks of turkeys each year, one in April for the Thanksgiving market and one in June for the Christmas market. Our April flock had been started in the small brooder houses and we looked forward with great expectations to brooding our June poults in the new building. The poults arrived and I monitored them as closely as a mother hen, making sure everything was perfect so that they would get a good start in life.

But, at about five days of age tragedy struck and more poults than usual started dying. This continued for the next 10 days with the lost of 1,000 poults. We tried everything we could to stop their deaths and called in disease experts but no one could come up with a cause.

We had made a large investment in the facility and since turkey growing was a large portion of our income it was critical that we solve the problem. In an attempt to solve the problem before starting our next year's crop, we ordered 2,000 poults, from another source to arrive in August. The same thing happened to these poults, only worse, about one-third of them died.

There seemed to be no solution. We thought we had checked everything. One advisor suggested taking a water sample for analysis but we replied that it had been tested earlier and had been using this well for six years. It was a little salty but had never bothered the turkeys. A sample was taken and sent to the lab for analysis. The report came back that the salt level in the well was very high and toxic to all animals, including turkeys. We located another well, had the water tested and grew the succeeding flocks successfully.

It was a quirk of fate that for some reason the well, that was only slightly salty and had been used successfully for several years, suddenly increased its salt level at exactly the time we started brooding poults in the modern new building. It is another example to prove Murphy's Law, "If anything can happen, sometime it will!"

*Circa 1955. New 8,000 square foot brooder house, which replaced a number of 12 x 14 foot brooder houses. This is the building where we proved 'Murphy's Law'. We were extremely proud of this building. We constructed it mostly with our own labor, as we did for another 25 years, and it was the 'state of the art' for 1955.*

# Precious Water

Most of us in Central NY think of water as something that is always available whenever we want it. That wasn't the case at Plainville Turkey Farm. There is no public water and for some reason our geologic underground has very little water. Even when I was a boy in the 30s, I can remember my dad dynamiting a hole in the ground without finding water. He eventually made arrangements with a neighbor, who lived two miles away, to use his spring and draw water to the turkeys. In 1948, he drilled a well over 200 feet deep and only obtained a small flow of water, which a few years later turned salty and could not be used.

Turkeys drink a great deal of water and it takes an even greater amount processing the turkeys for market. There was no way I could increase the business without an adequate supply of water. We were so short of water, in the 50s, that I hired the Baldwinsville Fire Department to bring us a load of water each day the week before Thanksgiving.

Maynard Hencle was a good friend who was very successful dowsing for water. He would cut a small crotch stick from a fruit tree and whenever he walked over a vein of water the branch turned and pointed to the ground. I know he was very accurate because wherever he located water and dug down for it we always found a gravel vein with water exactly where he said it would be. The only problem was the veins were shallow and produced a small amount of water. Each vein would have been sufficient to supply a house but we needed a much larger quantity to supply our turkey needs.

I purchased some property adjacent to the Seneca River and employed an engineer to explore the cost of treating and pumping river water to the farm. The verdict was that it was not a practical long-term solution. From 1954 to 1970 I had eight different wells drilled and hired backhoes dig another six. We could only obtain enough water to take care of our immediate needs with never any surplus.

I had learned that there was a large aquifer extending from Gates Rd. about 10 miles to the east of Baldwinsville. In 1970, I obtained permission from Herbert Voorhees to drill for water on his farm and if successful, purchase property from him for a well. A geologist made soundings with a type of underground radar and assured me it was a good location for water. I asked my friend Maynard Hencle to dowse for water on the property and we drilled on the spot that they both agreed upon. We were successful at less than 40 feet deep! What's more it was good quality water, actually testing the same as the Baldwinsville water since it came from the same aquifer. Now we had to run a water line a little over a mile to our processing plant.

We ran a four-inch line to the farm thanks to some good advice by another old friend, Clifford Lamb. Cliff also said, "Bob build a large water storage at the farm because there will be occasions when you will lose electrical power at the well or have the pump malfunction." I followed his advice and today, 40 years later, the well, pipeline and reservoir are still performing perfectly! I drink water from that well daily and continually realize how precious water can be.

# The Clergy

There is a joke, but one that is rather sad concerning a rural clergyman. The members of a rural church congregation were praying for a new pastor that was coming to their church. "Lord keep him humble, we'll keep him poor." Perhaps that phrase may have been part of the reason why three ministers helped my dad with the turkeys in the 30s and early 40s but I like to think it may have been over shadowed by the joviality and fellowship that was part of the work.

My dad was a man that worked hard but also loved fun. Jokes and stories were part of the everyday workplace. He seemed to make a game out of work, challenging people to race as they performed a task to determine who was the fastest. Of course, more work got done and the time passed more quickly.

Our normal farm work crew was about four people but at Thanksgiving time another 15 or 20 people were needed to catch the turkeys, prepare them for market and market them. Friends and neighbors either volunteered or were drafted along with two or three people who worked on farms by the day. This turkey processing group was a jovial gang, and the ministers were a big help and fitted in well.

For some reason the clergy always had the job of helping my dad prepare the turkeys for market after they had been bled and their feathers removed. They donned oilcloth aprons over their street clothes, were given knives and went to work. There was no running water and no sink to wash their hands.

After carrying a featherless turkey from the tobacco shed into the tobacco stripping room, where the turkeys were dressed, the first step was for each of the clergymen to take the turkey by its feet and put its head on a large wooden block. With a hatchet in the other hand, the head quickly dropped to the floor. Next, he took the turkey to the farm's workbench, which was now covered with oilcloth and removed the crop. The turkey was turned around and with a knife he removed the feet. Then he made a cut to remove the intestines, which were dropped into a garbage can along with the feet. The turkey was now ready for the consumer who would remove the giblets and clean the gizzard. A string was put around the turkey's drumsticks and it was again hung in the tobacco shed waiting to be bagged before heading to market.

With some religious faiths, animals and turkeys are blessed prior to slaughter. Our turkeys weren't blessed but were processed by happy people, including members of the clergy. Today professional people are often too far removed from the people that provide the physical work for necessary services. In looking back I believe that clergy, working with physical laborers at Plainville Turkey Farm, created a workplace environment that was beneficial for both.

*Circa 1954. Bob Bitz and his dog Trixie transporting water and feed to turkeys on pasture.*

# Hired Men in the 1930s

Our farm had only 96 acres of land until the 1940s but as long as I can remember we had a hired man. We had no tractor until the late 1930s so fieldwork was accomplished with horses. There was a small dairy herd and several labor-intensive crops, in addition to the turkeys. All of these enterprises required two hired men in addition to my dad. My father had worked as a hired man for other farmers when he was a young man and that experience provided him with the skills to interact successfully with his hired men.

Each spring the owner and the hired man came to a verbal agreement as to the expectations and remuneration for the forthcoming year. This agreement was seldom broken unless an unusual situation occurred. Some hired men stayed at a farm only a year or two, and then went to work on another farm hoping for a better situation. My dad's hired men and the ones, later, that worked for me usually stayed with us for many years.

A married man with a family was normally provided with a house, wood for heating and cooking, a quarter of beef and a hog at butchering time. Farms with dairy cows gave the hired man four quarts of milk a day and provided him with a plot for a garden. The cash wages were pitifully small, giving the hired man little hope of ever owning his own farm. I can remember helping move a hired man with his family to the farm in 1941. He received cash wages of $41 a month. There was also a single man who lived with our family. He received his room and board and about a dollar a day. Actually, at that time, many farm owners had difficulty making any profit.

The hours were long, starting at 5:00 a.m. and concluding at 6:00 p.m., six days a week. An hour was allocated for breakfast and an hour for dinner at noon, which was the big meal of the day. On Sunday, the hired men helped care for the cows and turkeys, which took about three hours. There was no vacation, pension or healthcare until the 1940s. If a man requested a day off for some special reason it was granted. Normally the hired man would be given a day to go to the fair and would still get paid if he were sick. Seldom did a hired man or employer feel bad enough not to work. It was a hard, disciplined life but no different than that of my father and the other neighboring farmers.

The relationship between farmer and hired man was a close, almost family like relationship. They worked together in a multitude of tasks almost every day. Spring was planting time, summer hay and grain harvest, fall potato and corn harvest and planting winter wheat. Much of the winter was spent in the woodlot cutting wood to be used by both employer and hired man the next year. Along with these seasonal tasks, the cows, horses and turkeys had to be cared for each day. You never saw a fat hired man! The hired man was an unsung hero. He worked hard, was paid little and received no recognition. His labor, however, was critical in producing food for millions of people.

# Nighttime Adventures in Dining

When I ask, what could be tastier than a Plainville turkey, an uninformed person might think it is a foolish question. I, however, can present evidence that will give the question credence for the previously uninformed.

What makes that question even more credulous is that the turkeys I am speaking of are still wearing their feathers and enjoying life. In addition, the variety of species enjoying Plainville turkey, make a solid case.

The first specie to be called to the witness stand is the wise old owl. Mr. Owl waits until darkness to enjoy his dinner, when his hunger pains cannot be further ignored. He flies to a high branch on a nearby tree where he can observe hundreds of Plainville turkeys, sitting on their roosts, enjoying a good nights rest. They are sleeping contentedly, after a busy day of stuffing themselves with corn and other goodies, getting themselves ready to be the centerpiece on a happy family's Thanksgiving dinner table. Mr. Owl's eyes travel, searching from one turkey to another, until finally unable to wait longer swoops down, with talons extended and beak ready, to enjoy his feast of the day. Proof that Plainville turkey is his culinary joy is that he returns night after night to satisfy his craving.

Our next witness is the cunning and crafty Mr. Fox. He holds a reputation as the nighttime visitor of the chicken house but few people realize that Plainville turkey is his heart's delight. He sniffs the night air, to make certain that neither man or dog is in the area. He then travels at a gentle lope, around the fenced turkey field, to determine where there might be either a hole in the fence or a space underneath to gain entrance to the smorgasbord of his dreams. He silently circles the turkeys in the field and stealthily approaches his choice for an early Thanksgiving feast.

Lest you think that it is only animals from the wild that savor Plainville turkey I must share with you the story of the gentleman who entered the turkey field in the middle of the night, secured a Plainville turkey and because he cared so much for it, he placed it next to him, on the seat of his pick-up truck. Impatient to start his feast, certainly not with a live turkey in full plumage, he decided to start with a beverage course. This first course, on a stomach still devoid of turkey, sent messages to his head that did not endear his driving to the village police.

Pursuit by the vehicle with the flashing red lights brought out his animal-friendly inner self. When apprehended by the policeman and asked why he had a live turkey next to him on the seat of his truck at that time of night, he responded, "my favorite turkey is sick and I am on my way to the veterinarian!"

Everyone who has been fortunate to enjoy Plainville turkey will recognize, however, that the driver of the pick up truck was not concerned with the health of the turkey but, like Mr. Owl and Mr. Fox, was willing to go to great extremes for the best in gourmet dining.

# Piles of Frozen Turkeys

We began further processing turkeys in 1958. Hens, ready for the oven, weighing 10-16 pounds were more popular with the consumer than toms, which weighed twice as much. As a result, we usually had surplus toms in the freezer long after the hens were all sold. We sold the extra toms to restaurants at a lower price than we were able to receive for the hens. To increase our profit we decided to provide an extra service for our customers by removing the bones and selling boneless meat, even cooking some of the meat.

The market was ready for turkey that could be prepared conveniently and it solved our surplus tom problem. We had, however, created additional problems. We showed customers the convenience of boneless and cooked products, now they wanted to buy these products all 52 weeks of the year. At that time our farm was set up to process whole turkeys from only October to April. Previously we had been freezing a few hundred extra toms but now we boned and sold that many in a month. How could we supply our customers the other five months?

One solution would be to construct more growing buildings and process live turkeys 12 months of the year. To do this would have required the investment of hundreds of thousands of dollars, which we didn't have. To solve the problem we employed the "poor man's" solution; solving the problem with the expenditure of as few dollars as possible.

The solution was three-fold like each leg on a three-legged stool. First, increase production 5-10% a year, as we could afford it. Second, limit our sales to what we could afford to produce. The third leg was to build enough freezer space to supply turkeys for further processing when we were not processing live birds. Freezer space is expensive so we built only what was absolutely needed.

We constructed a freezer 24 by 40 feet and 14 feet high. If we were to use pallets to store the turkeys on, the freezer would have held about 2,000 turkeys. By stacking the turkeys like cord wood we could store almost 10,000 in the freezer. Each turkey was put in a plastic bag and were never piled more than three high each day. Each turkey was exposed to the blast of cold air and frozen before additional layers were added. By carefully piling one on top of the other and slanting the pile to the back of the freezer we were able to pile 16 birds high. We never had a pile fall down and the system worked perfectly.

I was never too popular when I recruited workers to pass the turkeys up to me while I piled them. When the pile was near the top of the freezer it took three people, with one tossing the turkey up to the next one in line. Removing the turkeys we used the same system in reverse but in this case it was critical not to drop a frozen turkey on your foot or fingers. We wore clean rubber boots when we stood on turkeys for piling the upper rows. Eventually we purchased a conveyer with a rubber belt to elevate the turkeys to the top and only two people were required.

As I look back upon the process and the many piles of turkeys I marvel that we accomplished what we did, while always minimizing expenses. It is another example of the old adage, "necessity is the mother of invention."

A stack of thousands of large tom turkeys stored to be used for boning when there were not any live turkeys large enough to process. The turkeys were placed in plastic bags with about 200 piled each day to allow the previous day's turkeys to freeze before others were piled on top. When boning, about 100 were removed each day and thawed in water prior to boning and being turned into processed turkey products.

# Turkey Fries

The pork industry is known to use every part of the hog but the squeal. The turkey industry had never been able to equal that efficiency, until recently, but years ago I attempted to utilize as much of the turkey as possible. In addition to the whole dressed turkeys, we sold feathers to NY City feather merchants, manure to lawn and garden stores and turkey heads to mink farmers. Generally my attempts to market an unusual item met with failure because of small volume combined with the corresponding lack of marketing dollars. Attempting to market a new product was enjoyable, even though it didn't result in profits.

In the 1970s, we marketed many of our tom turkeys when they weighed over 30 pounds and were sexually mature. When these large toms were processed, we removed the testicles, which were in the body cavity, along with the intestines and threw them away. I had heard that there were food connoisseurs who enjoyed testicles from other animals and were willing to pay a premium price for them. If that was the case, why not market turkey testicles to be sautéed or fried and then served as turkey fries.

Each spring we took all of the farm's employees out to dinner at a popular restaurant. The year we started marketing the fries, we took them to a German restaurant where the owner was the head chef. He happily offered to serve the fries as an appetizer for our group. About half of our people tried the fries and two or three said how good they were but the handwriting was on the wall; our turkey fries were not going to be a run-away success.

Not to be deterred I decided to try to market them. The testicles from large tom turkeys are kidney shaped and about the size of a large strawberry, although white in color rather than red. When breaded and deep-fried there were a couple of mouthfuls from each one. We had a turkey product retail store on our farm so I filled a pint plastic container with about 20 testicles and offered them for sale.

We, of course, referred to them as turkey fries rather than testicles. People would ask, "What are turkey fries?" Their response after an explanation was usually, "Oh, I guess I don't care for any." Occasionally the response from a more adventurous person would be, "How do you cook them?" We would then explain that one successful method was breading and deep-frying. Seldom, however, did we find a buyer, even at the relatively cheap price of $4 a pint, for such a fine gourmet item. Every once in a while a real macho man thought they were the best food on earth, but this type of customer was far too scarce.

I take satisfaction in my failure to successfully market this product in that I was far ahead of the time for this fine product to be accepted; sadly most likely a time that will never arrive.

# Foie gras?

Plainville is located southeast of Lake Ontario, which is the big weather maker for our area. During the fall and winter the lake is often warmer than the air passing over it, and the air absorbs a large amount of moisture passing over the lake. As the air reaches land it is cooled causing precipitation in the fall as rain and in the winter as snow. This "lake effect" coupled with normal snowfalls provides our area with more than enough snow to make the residents happy.

Since the 1960s, we moved all of the turkeys from the fields to barns prior to December so as to not have them suffer outside in the cold and snow. Normally once this is accomplished the turkeys are comfortably housed and oblivious to the snow. Each building, housing the turkeys, had large feed containers holding a week's supply of feed, which was available for the turkeys to eat whatever they wanted, at all hours of the day. We never allowed the feeders to be totally empty, filling them when there was less than a day's supply remaining.

Weather forecasting was not as dependable or as accurate 50 years ago as it is today, and sometimes 'old man winter' played tricks on the weatherman. One year in early March, a huge snowstorm with strong winds piled high drifts of snow and closed all of the roads for several days. We had one flock of 1,500 large toms that were ready to be processed. There was only a day or two supply of feed in the feeders. The snowstorm made it impossible to move them to the processing plant or to get feed to the building.

Our feed mill was less than a half-mile from the turkeys but the county highway between it and our turkeys was piled high with snow and impassable. This barn of large turkeys ran out of feed and they were hungry. Turkeys are something like little children, when they are hungry they are unhappy.

We removed the snow on our farm roads and as soon as the county snowplow came through, we fed the turkeys. They had only been without feed for a day but to see them go after the feed you would have thought they hadn't eaten in over a week. Turkeys, like other birds, have an expandable crop and when it is filled the crop will hold as much as a pound of feed. The turkeys ate the feed crazily and were so hungry they didn't know enough to stop until they couldn't hold another morsel.

The turkeys seemed no worse for their experience and about a week later we took them to the processing plant. The turkeys looked fine but we were surprised to see that their livers were very large, more than twice their normal size and a light cream color rather than the normal dark color. What was wrong? We had never experienced anything like this in over 40 years of growing turkeys.

Then a light flashed in my mind! I was familiar with the French practice of force-feeding geese to produce large cream-colored livers for foie gras. That was it! Our turkeys had force fed themselves! No we didn't start marketing foie gras but I did have a good excuse to purchase a snowmobile to prevent something like this from happening again, and well, maybe also to have some wintertime fun.

*Circa 1966. Bob Bitz with his son Mark Bitz on their new Polaris snowmobile. The snowmobile never did have to draw feed but did transport nearby employees to the farm and back to their homes when the road was closed for a day because of snow.*

# The Customer is Sometimes Right

"Bob, would you please take this call?" requested Sherri, my secretary. "There's a man on the phone who seems quite upset and is complaining that the turkey he purchased for Thanksgiving stinks."

I picked up my phone and politely requested, "May I help you, sir?"

"Yes you can! That dumb girl of yours can't seem to understand that your turkey, that I paid good money for, stinks and I want my money back."

"We might be able to do that sir but first I need to ask you a few questions. Where and when did you purchase the turkey?"

He responded, "At your store on the farm two days before Thanksgiving."

"We sell only fresh unfrozen turkeys, so did you keep it refrigerated until you cooked it?"

"Yes I did. We cooked it on Thanksgiving and when we ate it, the turkey was good but now it stinks."

"That's funny," I remarked. "What did you do with the leftover turkey?"

"We put it in the oven."

"You put your leftover turkey in the oven! When was that?"

"Thanksgiving day after we finished eating."

"When did it first start smelling?" I asked.

"We didn't notice it until Tuesday. We went away for the weekend and when we came back Tuesday and took it out of the oven to finish eating it, the damn turkey stunk. We threw it out."

"Sir, you just told me that you put your warm leftover turkey in your oven, left it in the unheated oven for five days, and that it smelled bad when you took it out."

"It didn't smell bad. It stunk. I want my money back!"

"Sir, you said the turkey was fine when you ate it on Thanksgiving. Any turkey would go bad when left in a warm room for five days. We try hard to accommodate our customers but frankly this was your fault and we will not refund your money."

"That's the last turkey we will ever buy from you. You cheap skates! You'll be sorry after I report you to the police!"

Needless to say we never heard anything from the police or from this man again. It just goes to show that the customer is only sometimes right!

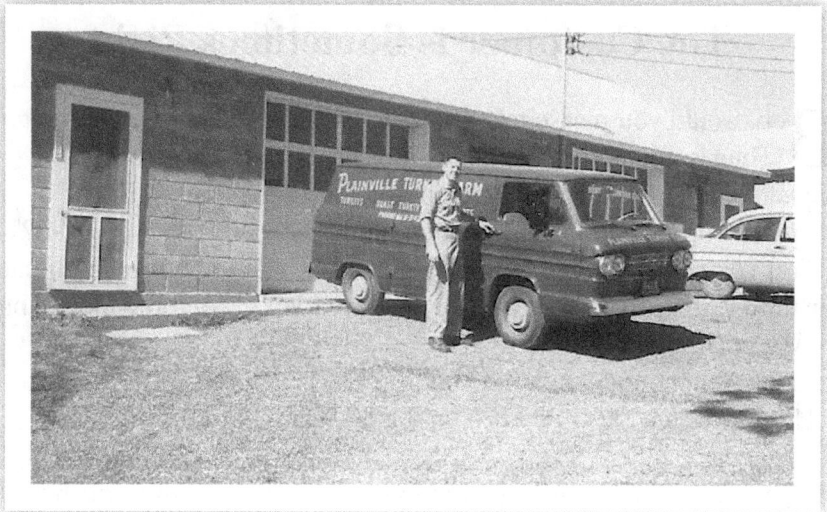

*Circa 1962. This Chevrolet Corvan is the first delivery truck the farm had to deliver its products to restaurants and stores. The business was much smaller at that time and we had three or four delivery routes each week. We called the customers on Monday to obtain their needs for the week.*

# Are Turkeys Polish?

"We would like you to host a Polish 4-H exchange student for six months," a person heretofore unknown to me, said on the phone. He was a Cooperative Extension representative from western NY looking for a turkey farm on which to place a student. "This student is a young lady who obtained a degree in poultry husbandry in Poland and wants to learn about turkey growing. We have been looking for a turkey farm and we need your help."

My wife and I had three children, one of whom had just married and left home, a second who was away in college and a third who was in high school. We had plenty of room in our home but were not really interested in increasing the size of our current family. I responded, "We would rather not. Can't you find another farm for her?"

"No, you are our last hope. She is used to working and you will find that she is a big help," he replied.

"Alright. When will she arrive?"

"You can meet her at the Greyhound bus station in Syracuse tomorrow morning at 11:00," he responded.

Janice, my wife, wasn't terribly pleased to have a Polish houseguest for six months but she has a very kind heart and gracefully accepted my decision.

The next morning my eyes roamed the bus station looking for someone that might be a young girl from Poland. A tall, slender, nice-looking blonde caught my eye. I wondered and secretly hoped that she was our guest. We approached each other and she asked in broken English, "Are you Mr. Bitz?"

"Yes," I smilingly responded, "You must be Leokadia. Welcome."

"Please call me Lou. It is much easier to say," she replied with a smile.

We rode 20 miles back to my home on the farm and Janice welcomed her. Since she had told us she wanted to care for live turkeys, the following day I put her to work helping one of my employees take care of thousands of turkeys in several large barns. After she learned our farm's procedures we placed two barns of turkeys in her care. For several months, as the turkeys grew from small poults into large toms, Lou cared for the turkeys both morning and night.

Finally, the time for marketing the turkeys arrived. On our farm, the live turkeys were driven, similarly to cattle but without horses and dogs, from the growing barns to the processing plant. Several of our employees and Lou were driving the turkeys but the turkeys were stubborn and extremely difficult to move. All of a sudden Lou walked up in front of the turkeys and started to talk to them. As she moved forward the turkeys followed her the rest of the way into the processing plant. This flock of turkeys moved the easiest of any of the flocks we had ever grown. I asked Lou what type of magic she used and she replied, "I just talked to them in Polish!"

*Circa 1953. In the background is the old tobacco shed that was used for processing turkeys until 1950. The farm still had dairy cows at this time and Bob's sister and family, visiting from Pennsylvania, are helping unload some second cutting hay.*

# Bulk Feed

As the number of turkeys we grew gradually increased from the early 1950s, the amount of feed they consumed increased proportionately. Handling innumerable tons of feed in 100-pound bags was beginning to be tiresome and we decided to change over to bulk feed.

We converted an old tobacco warehouse on our farm into overhead bulk bins on its 3$^{rd}$ floor and put in a used bucket elevator to fill the bins. We purchased an old truck and constructed wooden bins on it that had slanted bottoms to empty by gravity. By backing the truck into the converted tobacco warehouse we were able to fill its four bins by gravity. This was in the early 1950s and all of our turkeys were grown outside in fields. After filling the bins on the truck we drove it to the fields and used metal bushel baskets that filled by gravity from the bins in the truck, and then dumped the feed by hand into wooden feed troughs. We still had to lift the feed one time but had eliminated three earlier handlings of the feed. We also eliminated hundreds of bags that would have been needed to hold the feed.

At this time we were still buying feed from Beacon Milling Co. at Cayuga and we advised them that we were changing to bulk feed. They had never sold bulk feed but didn't want to lose our business so made arrangements for us to receive it in bulk. It was rather amusing to see how they provided the bulk feed. They put the feed in 100-pound bags as they always had and then when we came with our truck they untied the bags of feed and dumped the contents onto our truck. It took them about two years to modernize their methods and drop the feed on our truck from overhead bins.

We were still not satisfied with having to lift the feed even once. We decided to make some large feed troughs that each held almost one thousand pounds and purchased a power-take-off powered feed wagon, pulled by a tractor, to haul feed to our turkeys. By doing this we were able to eliminate all of the lifting and to take feed to our turkeys only once a week. This saved a great deal of time and effort with no detrimental effect to the turkeys.

Later we took automation in feed handling a step further when we began to grow our turkeys in buildings, by installing an automatic feeder in each building. The feeder was supplied by a large bin on the outside of each building. Now we were able to feed our turkeys and never lift a pound of feed or have to transport feed into the buildings.

Innovation, in the case of bulk feed, paid big rewards. It enabled us to feed more turkeys with less labor as well as lowering the cost of the feed by not having to purchase bags to put it in. All of the initial changes were made at minimal cost by using old buildings, second-hand equipment and improvising as needed to make changes that turned out successfully.

*Circa 1965. A picture of the old tobacco warehouse, on an adjoining farm we had purchased in 1952, that we refurbished for bulk feed. This picture was taken when our turkey production had reached more than 20,000 and we were making our own feed.*

# Soup's On

Remove the breast, neck, wings and legs from a turkey and what do you have? You have the makings for some delicious soup. Even when the breast meat and parts are removed with great care, the frame of the turkey, called the carcass weighs about 10% of the original live turkey and there is quite a bit of meat remaining.

I was brought up not to waste things and make as complete use of whatever I had as possible. In the early 1960s we were only boning about 80 turkeys a day but that meant we had over 200 pounds of carcasses each day with no use for them. My mother used to bring coffee to the processing plant employees at 10:00 each morning and when she saw that we were throwing the carcasses away she couldn't believe it. Never did she roast a turkey without making some delicious turkey soup from the carcass.

One of our valuable employees was a lady that had been trained at a culinary school. We asked her to experiment making a variety of turkey soups from the carcasses. She tried numerous recipes, which we all enjoyed sampling, and then we settled on a turkey rice soup.

Making soup from one carcass compared to making soup from 80 carcasses every day is a completely different ballgame. We needed to purchase a large steam kettle to cook the carcasses, develop a practical method of packaging and storage and develop a market for the end product. Our volume was small, which eliminated the possibility of purchasing expensive canning equipment so we decided to package the soup in pint containers and freeze it.

We designed and purchased pint cardboard containers, after receiving government approval of our labels, and purchased cartons to hold six pints of the turkey rice soup. Production began and now all we had to do was to sell it profitably.

In going out to sell soup to grocery stores I found that their buyers weren't exactly falling over each other to buy the soup. It took some persuasion and incentives to sell the soup. The soup took up space in their frozen food product displays and companies far larger than our little business were continually attempting to have the stores furnish them with more display space.

The soup was good but it was hardly selling. Thanksgiving was approaching and we decided to give a pint of soup to each turkey customer. Our turkey customers were loyal repeat customers and we thought if they tried the soup once they would want it again. Many of them did enjoy the soup and some purchased it again but it didn't have the addictive trait of nicotine and sales were few.

The turkey business is similar to a ballgame. There are always more outs than home runs and usually more outs than hits. Needless to say our adventure with turkey rice soup was a strike out. It turned out to be a costly venture with no return except for the realization that Plainville Turkey Farm was not Campbell's Soup!

# An April Fools' Joke

April Fool's Day has always been a significant day in our family. My
father enjoyed playing April Fools' jokes and taught me well, maybe
too well. I had some significant April Fools' jokes with my children but
since those jokes didn't involve turkeys, they will be omitted from this book,
which pertains to turkeys.

Our family has always had a close relationship, celebrating birthdays
and holidays. My daughter, husband and two granddaughters live 300
miles away so we often sent them a present in the mail. My granddaughters
were about nine and twelve at the time this soon to be described event took
place. A present from grandpa was always opened with anticipation and
glee, until after this particular April Fools' Day.

Both of my granddaughters enjoyed soccer and had played since they
were five years old. In soccer the feet and head are extremely important as
both are used to move the ball into the soccer net for a goal.

I grew up on a farm and the experiences on a farm bring one much
closer to animals and nature than my granddaughters' experiences living
in a suburb of Boston. As I created this joke, I based it on my background
while ignoring theirs. I also wanted to create a joke that they wouldn't
easily forget.

After locating an appropriately sized box, I placed my April Fools'
contents in the box and shipped it to arrive at their home on April Fools'
Day. The box was addressed to both of them and contained two similar
items for each granddaughter. Inside I wrote a note telling them that the

head and the foot were both a very important for winning in the game of soccer and that I wanted them to be winners.

Usually after a box arrives from grandpa his phone rings with joyful thanks for the gifts received. April Fools' Day came and went with no call. I realized that the mail might have been delayed but there was still no word from them several days later. Finally I called my daughter and asked, "Haven't the girls received a box from me?"

My daughter responded, "Dad, your April Fools' joke was gross. It totally freaked the girls out. We weren't even going to mention it. Yes, they received it!"

I could hardly imagine why my thoughtful gifts could freak them out. In reflection, I now realize some people might be surprised and bothered when opening a box containing two turkey heads and two turkey feet. I did receive some satisfaction, however, as 17 years have passed and they still remember those presents vividly!

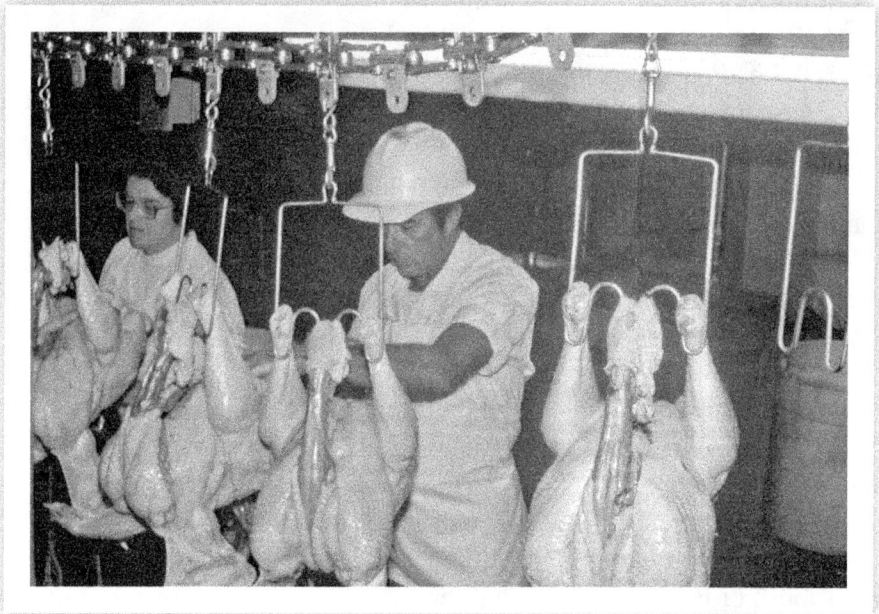

*Circa 1980. A picture of eviscerated turkeys being inspected by USDA Inspector Robert Dingman and valued Plainville Quality Control Inspector Janice Kline. The turkeys are hanging on a moving line with all stainless steel equipment, a stark contrast to production methods 40 years earlier.*

# Let's Build a Restaurant

It was always my goal to keep as much of the consumer's dollar as possible by eliminating middlemen. On the farm we were now boning, cooking and selling turkeys and turkey products retail. To me, the next step was to put the turkey on the customer's plate and eliminate another middleman by building a restaurant.

I knew nothing about the restaurant business but my wife Janice had a cousin, Victor Johnson, who owned a successful fast food restaurant and had previously sold some of our turkey products. I talked with him about the possibility of forming a partnership and opening a fast food turkey restaurant. He thought it might be a good idea. To be certain we were on the right track I set up a meeting with an agricultural economics professor, Stan Warren, who I admired and had taken classes from when I was at Cornell.

Stan invited Professor Max Brunk, who specialized in marketing, to join us. Victor and I explained what we had in mind. We were going to feature Plainville turkey, serve it fast food style, hire a manager and give McDonald's some competition. Stan and Max asked quite a few questions and then gave us their opinion. They said with absentee ownership, lack of previous experience, the competitive nature of the restaurant business and featuring turkey, which was mostly a Thanksgiving and Christmas meat, it would not be wise to open a restaurant.

Now that we had received some knowledgeable advice we decided to go ahead and build a restaurant anyway. We scoured the countryside around Syracuse and decided on a site near Cicero and Route 81. We purchased a four-acre plot of ground that had previously been a dairy farm. In fact, we pushed over a silo that was still standing and filled in the barnyard around it. Victor and I served as general contractors, and hired a number of very fine people as sub-contractors. We started the project in November and opened the restaurant the following August, 1973. General contracting a restaurant brought many new experiences but we survived them all.

We learned a great deal! Customers didn't want to eat turkey from paper plates, they wanted the whole turkey not turkey rolls, employees were not always perfect and we weren't always accurate in analyzing our managers. We persisted, made changes to please our customers and began to move away from red ink on the bottom line. About 15 years later Victor and I dissolved the partnership amicably, and I was swimming alone.

The business prospered and we actually had customers drive from Canada and many other distant points to eat at the restaurant. We made a number of additions to the restaurant and quadrupled the seating. It became a destination point for travelers and was a busy place, especially during the summer and fall.

One day, after we had been open about 25 years, I made one of my twice-weekly stops at the restaurant. I happened upon Max Brunk and his wife in the crowded restaurant enjoying a turkey dinner. We exchanged pleasantries and Max looked me in the eye and said, "Bob, I have to admit that when you came to see Stan and myself about the advisability of opening this restaurant, we gave you some poor advice."

# Necessity is the Mother of Invention

During December and January in 1955, we still had turkeys on what had been pasture, months earlier, but now resembled Santa's North Pole. It was not only a difficult life for the turkeys but was expensive for us because the feed that they consumed was being used to maintain their body temperature rather than adding meat to their bodies. We knew the turkeys should be in a building protected from the winter's cold and snow, but buildings cost money and there was a lot more snow than money available.

Pole barns were a relatively low cost new type of barn being constructed on farms at that time. We had a woodlot on the farm and thought that if we cut some logs to saw into lumber we might lower the cost of the building sufficiently to afford it. If we had some poles and constructed the building with our own labor, it was possible.

We learned that Niagara Mohawk Power Co. was replacing a power line along a road about 10 miles from our farm. What were they going to do with the poles they were replacing? We made some inquiries and found that they had no use for the old poles and that we could have them. They would let us know when we could obtain the poles. We thanked them and said in appreciation for their courtesy we would see they received a ready-for-the-oven Plainville turkey. Our problem was now partially solved.

We went to the woods and turned a number of hemlock trees into logs of the appropriate lengths we needed and transported them to a nearby sawmill. Shortly thereafter we received a call telling us that the poles were ready to be picked up along the roadside. Our farm labor force consisted of four men, which included my dad and myself. We took a farm wagon, tractor and chainsaw to retrieve the poles.

The poles were huge and heavy. When driving by a power line, supported by wooden poles, the poles do not look very big but when you are lifting them on a wagon, by hand it is a different matter. Some were as large as 14 inches in diameter and even though we cut all of the poles into 12 and 16-foot lengths, they were about all we could handle. The poles had been in the ground for many years but were still in good condition.

The bottom six feet of each pole had been pressure treated. The top portions of the poles, where we had cut them, were going to be placed in the ground so I needed to treat them with a rot preventative. To do this I fashioned a tank six feet high and used rope and pulleys to lift them up and let them down into the tank where they sat two days for treatment.

During spare time in the summer we constructed the building, having to buy only the sheet metal roofing, nails and wire for the sides. When December came our turkeys were all under cover and we were very happy. Of course, the turkeys had no idea of the efforts we put forth to provide them with a more comfortable residence for their remaining days. When the turkey business was sold 51 years later, the building was still in good condition and the poles looked like they could last another 50 years.

*Circa 1956. This building was constructed very economically by sawing lumber from the farm's woodlot, using free, old electric light poles to support the frame and using farm labor during a slow time of y ear. Pole buildings like this made life for our turkeys more enjoyable in inclement weather. This barn is still in good condition.*